SEE BENEATH MY SMILE

The Beginning of Your Story
Doesn't Dictate the Ending

SIMONE D. BAILEY

TABLE OF CONTENTS

DEDICATION

This book is dedicated to my adopted dad.

Thank you for always believing in me.

You supported whatever I did no matter what and this would not have been any different.

May you rest in peace.

PROLOGUE

HOW WOULD YOU LIVE YOUR LIFE
WITHOUT A BIRTH CERTIFICATE?

HOW WOULD YOU BE ABLE TO TRAVEL
WITHOUT A PASSPORT?

IF YOU DON'T KNOW WHEN YOUR BIRTHDAY IS, WHEN
WOULD YOU CELEBRATE IT? OR WOULD YOU?

YOU HAVE NO PARENTS; THEY ABANDONED YOU AS AN
INFANT. HOW DO YOU NAVIGATE WITHOUT A FAMILY?

DO YOU TRY TO GO OUT AND FIND THEM
WITH ZERO INFORMATION… LIKE A BLIND
DETECTIVE? OR SIMPLY MOVE ON?

SIMONE wanted to know these answers. She wanted a real family… her birth family, and answers to the real questions about her life that have left her empty with a huge question mark for most of her life.

Questions like why life, and the world, was so difficult. Foster care, sexual abuse, beatings, adoptions, emancipation all before the age of 16. And still, no answers.

And at 18, she got a file of papers with more questions than answers.

Over twenty years later... after travel, hours upon hours on the phone with various people, walking the streets with flyers, years of day-to-day research, and a lot of money spent... she has finally answered most of the questions, but two.

Join her in this 20+ year ongoing saga to find her family, and herself.

CHAPTER ONE

....

Introduction

Twenty years... I don't know for sure. It may be more than twenty years... maybe 25 years. I have been thinking, wondering, then asking and looking, for my 'real' family. My blood family, family who looks like me. You know, if I took a DNA test it would say those two people ARE my flesh and blood, biological parents. With 'real' biological brothers, sisters, cousins... you know, a real family full of people who are all blood related.

Yes, I am adopted. Ok, I WAS adopted, and for 'reasons' became emancipated at age 16, by the court. Life was never easy; most of the time it was barely tolerable. Some of these stories will upset you, too. They were even harder to have to relive them while writing this book. I was the one who lived through these experiences and had to survive them.

I was born to my biological parents, this much I know, but then it gets fuzzy. A litany of people and places and snippets of memories, until I finally have a memory or two, but by then a few years had passed and how I wound up where I was, I had no clue.

So, when I turned 18, I got a copy of my adoption file and started reading and digging, digging and reading, looking for answers about my fractured life, and it hasn't stopped since, close to twenty five years later. I keep finding pieces of information... pieces of my life. I get closer to closure every year and then, poof... one dead end (literally) after another... and then sometimes I get lucky. Other times I have to get tough... it is my life after all, and I am entitled to know what happened, who was involved, and where I came from and who I am.

It wasn't easy for me living these years, so I can't say enjoy the reading. It is raw. It is real. It is my life.

Calissa-Simone

CHAPTER TWO

··

My Earliest Memories

The earliest memory I have of my childhood is being attacked by a dog. I was in a motel room. I was somewhere between the ages of, maybe two and four, and was sitting cross-legged on the bed. I remember this man who was lying next to me. He was laying completely straight, flat out. I remember there being a woman in the room; she left the room for a short while, and all of a sudden this huge and very angry dog jumps on the bed. I didn't realize the dog was in the room. I remember just sitting on the bed, playing with a little doll. Then the dog jumps on the bed and immediately starts attacking us, the man and me.

At the time, I didn't realize the man couldn't really move. I later found out that he was a quadriplegic, paralyzed from the neck down. He was yelling; he was screaming. He was trying to move his body, but he couldn't really do much to protect me. I remember yelling and screaming and trying to fight this dog off me. And the dog is just constantly biting me and biting me and biting me. I didn't know what to do. It felt like something out of a horror movie and I wasn't sure how I survived. Eventually, I fell off the bed and the man fell off the bed. I guess there were people outside the motel room who heard the commotion going on, and they called the cops.

I was taken to the hospital and evaluated, and of course, social services got involved because I was just a little child, and the man wasn't able to protect me. So there was a case of neglect. The woman came back and saw the craziness going on. The police questioned her as well, but after the police and social services left the hospital, the man and woman were able to take me away, and fled the state due to pending neglect charges. How they were able to abscond with me and get away, I have no clue, but this was happening all over New York and other places as well.

But this led down a path of who am I? Who are these people? I don't belong to these people. That's what it really boils down to. I end up going into social services. So that's one of the earliest memories I have of myself... being attacked by a vicious dog. That's my first memory of being a child, and what's crazy is when I was attacked by that dog, as I was growing up from there, I really didn't remember it.

I didn't put two and two together until I turned 18 and got a copy of my adoption file. I saw the case and it references the dog attack and how social services got involved in all this. So it's really interesting from that particular age up until I was 18, I just had bad nightmares about being attacked by a dog. The body kept repeating the feelings, but the mind wouldn't permit the connection. Any time I would walk down the street and I heard a dog, I was terrified, and never knew where that came from, or why, until age 18 and then, oh, 'I was attacked by a dog'. Sounds simple enough, but try going through it for 13 or 14 years without a clue. Just an abject fear of dogs.

I remember being told I was born in New York. Right now, it's believed to have been at Bronx Lebanon Hospital, but I am still looking for my birth certificate. Yes, after more than twenty years of searching and investigating, I am in my forties now, and have no birth certificate. Simple enough... but the hospitals, county records offices, state birth certificate offices, medical offices, US Passport office, don't have it either. There aren't that many hospitals to search there, so I did... but no one seems to have any records of me? Why, after all these years, am I still looking for my birth certificate?

Somehow, I ended up with this black man and white lady. They were not my biological family, but I ended up with them and went on this countrywide tour with them. The woman was 'wanted' for many other things... the usual laundry list for small time crimes. She stole people's identities, distributed narcotics, falsified documents (including my birth certificate, baptism certification, prescriptions for medications, etc.) So I eventually went into state protective custody in Oklahoma City. Some of the earliest memories I have are when I was in Oklahoma, in different foster homes there. I can't even remember how many foster homes or what ages I was; I just remember these various homes with kids and different adults there and trying to understand what was going on.

Major Roberson. He was a black man who was in my adoption file. Whenever I came into his care, he was with a white lady, and for the sake of simplicity, I'm gonna call her his wife. Her name was Betty Roberson and they were in a relationship. But as I said, he was already quadriplegic in a wheelchair, although I really didn't have a concept of that as a child. I remember him always speaking really nice to me, and being nice to me. And I remember the white lady, Betty, not really knowing who she was, but her being nice to me as well. I don't really remember any negative experiences with either of them, other than the dog attack.

How I got into the care of Major and Betty Roberson, I have no idea. I have some assumptions. And my assumptions start with my biological father, whose name is Clarence Cross. Somehow, maybe he came in contact with Betty and Major. I feel like it was more so Betty, because my father was a big drug kingpin in New York. I believe he and Betty had some drug business together.

Another assumption that might have happened... After connecting with my biological sister, our mom left me with this couple as she frequently left my sister and me with various people in the neighborhood, or should I say 'babysitters', while she went off for her 'fun'. Being left with babysitters was something that happened quite often. And not just for a few hours, but days upon days! That is how social services would get involved at times because we were left with these babysitters and our mom would not come back for days. Potentially, I was left with a babysitter and Betty and Major took off with me. When my sister and mom came back for me, I was gone and they never saw me again. My sister and I reconnected early in 2023, so this is where the assumption came from, but I am not sure I will ever know the truth.

At any rate, my biological mom, because she was heavy on the drugs that I assume my biological father gave her; she couldn't care for me. I believe she kept harassing my father about needing drugs, needing money, and needing help to take care of me. And I believe my mom gave me to my father, and my father gave me to Betty and Major to take care of me, and to this day, my biological father has not had a conversation with me about the situation.

I truly believe my father was expecting this situation would never resurface. I mean, it has taken a couple decades for me to get this deep, and know what I know. And now that it has resurfaced and I have found him, that is not something he wants to address, or he wants to face, or he wants to deal with. So that's another story.

Major ended up passing away from his injuries and his health conditions overall, from being paralyzed from a car accident. Betty was a very interesting character. She was a little drug lord on the streets. She sold a lot of prescription medication belonging to Major. As mentioned previously, she also forged a lot of prescriptions. She took peoples' identities and had multiple warrants out for her arrest. And I only 'say' Betty Roberson because it's taken me a long time to find this lady, because I wasn't certain whether or not the name Betty was her actual real name. And I'm not sure if I completely found her, but what I have found is that she is deceased. She passed away in 2015.

My dad, my biological father, is not willing to discuss with me about these people, about my mom, about anything. I will get to him at some point in the story.

I do my best to remain calm in the face of ignorance; I keep a straight face and have attempted to contact him for more information... many times. But, frankly, I often think of beating him up until he tells me everything I want to know. He has not contributed a dime or a hello in all these years, and I owe him some of the pain I have had to endure because he has been unwilling to take responsibility for his actions. It was more than forty years ago and all I am asking for is answers. No money, no support, not even a Kleenex for the tears I shed... just answers.

I'm assuming I entered foster care after Betty was apprehended by law enforcement. She had a criminal record that was following her and she ended up being incarcerated, then I went into the foster care system in Oklahoma. And because there was no real record of who I was or where I came from, I went into the system through social services based on what little was in my 'file' at the time.

The Department of Children's Services did some digging. They did some work with researching and reaching out to some of Major's family members; some of Betty's family members. Everyone said Betty was a habitual liar and she and Major just appeared with me one day out of nowhere. I ended up finding Major's family. I still interact with them to this day. I am good at connecting the dots, but there have been so many that became invisible, disappeared, that I am weary... tired of connecting. And now after over 20 years, I am exhausted... running on fumes... and not sure where or what dots to connect to next.

CHAPTER THREE

Woes of Foster Care

The next few chapters will detail a few of my foster care experiences. These weren't pleasant… they were far from that.

It's hard for me to identify what exact age I was with no actual birth certificate. So, trying to determine age was always done in a roundabout way until court documents of adoption were finalized. I definitely was at an age where I remember the school bus coming around and getting on the bus. So the main memories I have from this particular foster home and we're going to call this foster home 'the mobile home' was that there were boys in this home. There were boys and they were older. I could not have been older than seven. I only know this because one of the foster homes I went to later adopted me, and I was eight going on nine when I arrived at their home.

It wasn't a home that was completely built into the ground; that was very new for me as a child. I remember the wood paneling on the walls, and this little mobile home didn't have many windows; or they were always covered… it seemed like it was always dark. There were many kids in this home and I remember wherever this mobile home was; it was on a lot of land. You could just go outside and run in any direction for as long as you wanted to. The land was mostly just dirt. Red dirt or clay. I don't recall any other houses or trees. Like, literally no greenery anywhere. I remember there being kids there, some boys and some girls, different ages, and I felt like I might have been the youngest child at this home. Of course there were foster parents, but I hardly remembered them. The only memory of the foster parents I had was when they were preparing for a birthday party. Not sure whose party it was but it was a big day.

And that was one of the, I don't want to say, worst days of my life, but that was one of the days I can very vividly remember being sexually abused. And I remember one of the boys telling me to lick his ear and I was just like, lick your ear? What does that even mean? But as I'm licking his ear he was obviously satisfying himself. I don't have a whole lot of fond, early memories. Without talking much about 'the system' it is easy to see 'the system' wasn't working. Sexual abuse was repeated at every foster home unfortunately. It was like I could not get away from it and it really impacted me as a young adult. It is very unfortunate that 'the system' that is supposed to protect you, is the one doing the most harm.

I eventually left that foster home because there were continued instances of sexual abuse. The foster parents seem to have been really nice people, but I think with all the kids, it definitely felt like it was an overly full home. Not really having a place to sleep. Not really a clean environment. I remember bugs and cockroaches crawling on me, anywhere I slept in that house. And then I just remember the boys, always forcing me to do different things so they could please themselves. It wasn't always the 'typical' definition of abuse... much of it was, "do this for me, and I will do the rest", and they would be getting themselves off on whatever they told me to do. Somehow, I got out of that house, thank God.

You can use your imagination, but there were things that a little girl should not be doing, at any age. I should not have been anywhere near their pants, licking their ears, their necks, or for that matter me touching them anywhere, and them touching me anywhere. It was disgusting. And not only that, I had to deal with these boys any time they had a moment they felt like no one was going to be looking or watching; they would behave like that. I don't even know if they did this with the other girls. I don't remember the other kids being around. These boys always found a way, with such a full house, to arrange the situation to be them and only me, with no one else around.

The foster mom would never yell at us; she never asked us to clean up or clean the kitchen or clean the house. I don't remember anything like that. Not to say it didn't happen, but I just remember the whole house was always a mess. We didn't spend much time in the house anyway. We were always outside running around in the dirt.

Another foster home experience I had definitely impacted me as well. I remember this home; it was a beautiful home. The back yard was beautifully manicured because I remember enjoying playing outside in the grass. I remember the playground set they had out there. I remember the kitchen and the island in the center. I remember a hallway that was like a raised hallway where you walk down the middle and, on both sides, it was like a step down, and you went into a living room area, or maybe it was a den.

There was another child with me in this home and this child was not a foster child; I believe it was their biological child.

Interestingly enough, I can't remember if it was a boy or girl, but it was a difficult situation. It was too hard for me to focus on the gender of the other child, but I just remember there was a very strong difference in how I was treated versus how this other child was treated.

This was the home that started me down the path of stealing food. I remember the adults cooked often. I remember the foster mom always baking goodies like cookies and bread, along with other things, and there was always food in the refrigerator and candy bowls filled to the brim, but unfortunately, I could never have any of that. So I would steal the food. I would sneak in the kitchen and steal the things I could get my hands on quickly. Now keep in mind these parents, I do not recall them ever laying a physical finger on me.

But their form of punishment was something maybe even more traumatic. Everybody would be eating their food and they only fed me two items in this home… oatmeal and beans. And I would eat it because I was hungry. That was all I had. And I remember those white beans, they were disgusting. The oatmeal wasn't so bad, but the white beans made me sick to my stomach, but I ate them because that's all I was given. White beans, I believe they were hominy beans and they were terrible.

So instead of eating the oatmeal and beans three times a day and being sick, there were times I would steal cookies and other food. I would come in from playing and sneak around the house when going to the bathroom and take whatever I could that was quick; cookies, candy, bread, anything! It was better than beans and I was willing to take the risk to have something other than that.

And every time I snuck food I was punished and their form of punishment was making me stand in the garage. Before I stepped foot in the garage, I would have to take off all my clothes, my underwear, dress shoes, anything I had on. I remember the foster mom would come with a pitcher of ice-cold water and would pour the ice cold water over the top of my head and it would run down my body and she would leave me there; and depending on how they felt, I guess the level of punishment would determine how long I stayed out there. Sometimes it was for a few minutes, other times for hours, and sometimes, all night long.

I remember trying to sleep close to the cars because there was a little bit of heat that would come from the cars. Especially if the car had been driven that day, it would be a little warmer. I would curl up by the vehicle, on the concrete, and go to sleep. I would lose track of time and it seemed like I was out there for hours upon hours, and sometimes I was. And this was my punishment for stealing food in their house.

Cold water poured on my head traumatized me so badly that even as an adult I cannot stand water to be poured or splashed on me. Those rain showers that everyone loves, nope. I can't stand rain showers. It automatically takes me to a pitcher of cold water being poured on me. It was the worst; it was the absolute worst. I do hope these foster parents know they scarred me for life. I wish I knew who they were and could have a conversation with them, but I hope they eventually got what they deserved.

I remember when social services would come check on us in the house and I would speak up, but people would think I was lying, or they would make it out like I was making up stories. "Oh, she's such a storyteller." Abuse? Torture? If I spoke up it would have been worse… being called a liar and being sent to juvenile detention instead of in a decent home.

At the mobile home, I remember when social services came out there and telling them about the boys and what they had me do. At the time I didn't think it was anything bad, I just knew I didn't like doing it. No one believed me and it got to a point where I was experiencing all these things, so I thought this was normal. And I didn't want to share or talk about what I was going through, so I just stopped talking. I remember people telling me all the time things like, "you have no emotions, you have no facial expressions. You don't even swing your arms when you walk. There's something wrong with you". And really what was wrong with me were the things I had to experience in some of these foster homes that were just traumatic to me. And when that trauma builds without any release, or even an acknowledgement that what I was saying was true… it quickly became a case of survival. Keep your head down, say nothing, stay alive, and count the days, weeks, months, and years until the situation changes.

So let's move on to a different foster home, where clothes were always secondhand and shoes weren't a necessity. If I wore shoes, they either were so small that my feet hurt so bad I would rather be barefoot, or there was never any food in the house. So, I stole food when we would go to the store. I literally just would steal every chance I got because I wasn't sure where my next meal was gonna come from.

But I was in a home that was supposed to provide food, clothing, and shelter. I think I got the shelter at this home, but the food and the clothes and other stuff, I just don't remember. All the other children in the home were bad, like very bad. I knew I did not belong there and I had to get the hell away from that home. It was rough having to steal food and get clothes and shoes from wherever I could. I don't even remember toys or even having the time to play with toys. Can you believe I wasn't even eight years old and I had no time for toys! My focus was on survival only and trying to make it through.

The last foster home I was in was supposed to be my forever home… and it actually ended up being the home where they adopted me. So, this particular foster home was in Oklahoma City. A husband and wife couple, and they typically would have five to six foster kids in their home. I remember coming to their house and hanging out with all the other kids. I remember it might have been the social worker telling me that this family wanted to adopt me. And that meant I wouldn't have to go anywhere else ever again. That this would be the last home and I was okay after experiencing the horrors of all these other homes.

Now, keep in mind the home I went to where they were pouring cold water on me in the garage, they allegedly wanted to adopt me, too. But I'm not sure what happened there, but needless to say, I was glad to get out of there. Every home I left; I was glad to leave. So now I'm at this house and I remember there were two boys. I remember the two boys and that they were planning to adopt one of those boys and maybe one of those boys was their child, maybe? I remember the back yard which was like a fun playground. Lots of play sets and tree houses and basketball nets. And so it was always a fun time. We played all day, all night. But I remember this house being very, very strict. The foster dad, he worked long hours. But when he was around, he was very loving, very attentive, and played with all of us. The mom was around most of the time but there was no bond.

So, I remember being in this home for a little while and then for some reason I left that home for a bit too, but I don't know why. And when they brought me back to this home, I remember them saying, "now we're going to adopt you and asking would I like to be adopted, and what would I like my name to be?" Because, keep in mind, and I have not even mentioned this... The name I entered into the foster care system was actually Calissa Roberson. I was carrying on the last name of that family from New York, Major and Betty's last name. And Calissa was the name they were calling me.

I remember the day the adoption took place and we went to court. It was me, the other little light-skinned boy, and the parents. The light-skinned boy was also adopted on the same date as I was. I remember the last thing the social worker said to me, "This is now my forever home and family."

I want to talk about this home because now I am in a decent space with this family. But we went through a whole lot of shit. So first, let me just give the childhood experiences with them. And when they adopted me, they changed my name to Simone Danielle Branham, which was their last name. I remember them asking me what did I think about this name, but I'm just the kid so you know, it was okay. They picked out a birthdate for me as well. And when all those things were established and in place, the adoption was finalized. There were many issues with my adoption, which I didn't know about until later. And I say issues because no one knew where I really came from. There was discussion of me being a 'stolen child.'

But they were able to adopt me, and I remember being in school and my name going from Lisa to Simone, and I remember there were kids who actually remembered my name. I was called Lisa, short for Calissa. One asked, "hey, I remember your name used to be Lisa, and now it's different?"

As I reflect on this home, it was good. You know, there was definitely some abuse on all levels, but because this was my 'forever' home (or so I thought), I endured. The trauma I had already experienced previously was heavy. PTSD was present.

No one had given me any real security. No one had given me that safety net. It was always very short lived. I have to admit, some love and attention, positive attention, would have helped me immensely both physically and mentally, as well as emotionally. But unfortunately, it wasn't meant to be. The goal was to get through this and hope the next phase of life would be better.

CHAPTER FOUR

····································

Forever Home

I was already way down the road with my bad habits of stealing and lying, and just keeping to myself. I was very much on edge because no adult had taken good care of me, or ever really gave a damn about me, that much I do remember. I didn't have fond memories. I guess you could call me 'paranoid', which made my transition to my forever home very challenging.

The 'system' is so broken that, even when an adoption takes place, the 'parents' have almost zero information about their new 'child', and the child has absolutely zero information about the situation they are entering into. This breeds mistrust, and the belief that all 'parents' are going to act like the stereotypically bad foster parents most kids have, over and over. And the new parents see all children from the system as dangerous and damaged, which we likely are, and to be handled like dynamite, not broken stuffed toys that really need love and affection. It all combines to make us kids less hopeful about our situation and future. Changing the process of the system with a fair amount of supervised communication would improve both sides for the long term. But, of course, I did not learn this until much, much later in life.

In my forever home I had two brothers; there was Michael who was adopted at the same time I was, and James, who we thought was their child at one point, but we later found out he was adopted as well. Because I was the oldest in this household, much of the weight of everything fell on me. The cleaning of the house, washing the dishes, the cooking, hell, just about any chore you could think of in and outside the house. Yeah, it felt like Snow White and the Seven Dwarfs, cleaning all the time. Everybody else got to have fun, but I couldn't. It was like I had to cook. I had to clean. I had to polish brass. I had to fold everybody's clothes, put everybody's clothes away, wash the dishes, prepare meals. Was I just adopted to be their slave? Like, really!

Now keep in mind, this is all at a very young age. I came to my forever home about the age of eight. I think they adopted me when I was like almost ten, based on the birthday they gave me. No one else in the house did the stuff I had to do. The adopted mom also cooked and cleaned, but no other kids did. It was like that was solely my job. And it was annoying, but I was happy to have clean clothes, to have good shoes on my feet, and to have food on the table that I could eat. I was really grateful since I never had any of these things before, but it came with a lot of sweat on my part.

It was really hard for me to enjoy those positive, happy moments that I did have. My adoptive mom and I were never on the same page. She wanted a mother and daughter relationship, but she sure had an odd way of showing it. I didn't like being in the same room with her because she was so mean to me. She was very verbally abusive. She would tell me how no one wanted me, or that I would not make it in the real world. She knew I would steal food, so she called me Miss Piggy instead of learning and understanding why I stole food. She knew I lied, but she didn't understand why I lied. When I shared with her that I was sexually abused and I didn't like people touching me, she didn't trust me or seek to understand. I truly did not understand why they had kids. These interactions with her made me hate her as a kid. I know hate is a strong word but that is how I felt as a kid, but of course, I don't feel that way now. I know many foster and adopted parents get into this field for the wrong reasons. I truly felt her reasons were the wrong ones, too.

More efforts should be placed on digging into the potential parents' trauma, and ensure they seek some type of counseling to prevent parents taking in children for the wrong reasons. I do believe my adopted mom's heart was in the right place, but she did not know how to give love. The saying of 'hurt people hurt other people', is very true but unfortunately, I did not learn this myself until I was much older.

My adopted mom was not the disciplinary parent. She would tell our father, our adopted dad, and he would go the fuck off on us. He would whoop us good. I can say whooping now, but back then it felt like a beating. Those whoopings left bruises. I had marks left on me numerous times, and going to school, being fair skinned and people seeing these bruises, always sparked issues and brought up questions. So it was an ongoing thing for us.

I truly believed that my adopted dad did things just to satisfy her. There was a lot of tension between the two of them which he took out on us. I mean, there were times when he would pick my brothers up, Michael and James, by their necks and shatter mirrors with their heads. I mean, it was bad at times. It actually got really bad. They believed in whooping their kids. If it wasn't a switch, it was a belt, and sometimes it was their hands. Or 'his' hands I should say. The crazy thing is, we were not bad kids either!

As much as I wanted to believe it was almost normal, deep down I knew better. Yes, I had seen this behavior in other foster homes and adoptive homes, but this was taken to a different level. This was supposed to be my forever home and now I am stuck in this mess. Being apprehensive and scared… no, being insecure and distrustful, was confirmed regularly.

After too many times of going to school with bruises and stuff on me, and social services being called out, I wanted out of this life. My adoptive parents eventually lost their rights to be foster parents.

They ended up removing all the other foster kids from the home but unfortunately, I remained.

After all this, it forced the adoptive mom to go outside the house and work which gave her even more ammunition for her to throw at me now that she had to go to work because I had "opened up my mouth" (her words). All I did was show up at school beaten half to death. Look, if they weren't busy changing my skin color every few weeks, this would have never happened.

Both parents were now outside the house working. The dad worked anywhere between 12 to 14 hour shifts typically, with very few days off. If the parents were not at home, we sat outside, did whatever until they came home because we were not given a key to the house. In the summertime we were told to stay in the house until they were home, so we didn't have a whole lot to do in the house, but we made do. One of the things we took advantage of was talking on the phone while the parents were gone. So it was fun while it lasted. We didn't have a phone in the house for us to use, even though there was a phone line, but we weren't allowed to use it, and the physical phone would be taken out of the socket so that we couldn't use it when they were not home.

So what does Simone the smart one do? Steal a phone from somewhere else and bring it into house, hide it, and use it when we want to use it, which was when the parents would be gone. When they found it, boy did we get in trouble. I hid the phone somewhere in the laundry or linen closet. The adopted mom found it and I didn't admit to bringing the phone home because I was scared. I knew it was only a matter of time before our dad came home and all hell would break loose. Sidenote, I have to actually thank my brothers because they very rarely ratted on each other, or me for that matter.

Back to hell… adopted dad came home and he went berserk on us that day. It got to a point where he lined us up in the living room, as no one had admitted anything about the phone, and he was picking us up by our necks. The boys didn't deserve this, and it was crushing me, so I finally admitted it was me. He sent the boys to their room and all I remember was him using the buckle part of the belt. Then at some point he puts the belt down, and now he's punching me. Punching me in the face and my body. There was blood everywhere. I could hear the boys crying from their room. Our adopted mom was in the house, but she refused to come out of her bedroom which was in the back of the house. When she did finally come out, the damage had already been done. I was on the floor. I remember the school shirt I had on; it was covered in blood. And now she's panicked and frantic. They're trying to figure out what they're gonna do with me because I'm curled up in a ball on the floor with a bloody fucking nose.

I remember my adopted dad leaving the house to calm down. I was sent to my room and they started trying to clean stuff up. I don't remember seeing my adopted dad for a few days; he was gone. And when he came back, he apologized. He apologized and said he was really sorry. Now, as an adult, I understand that abusers act like that. They go batshit crazy and then apologize, and wet their pants to get you to accept their apologies not turn them into the police. Back then, I thought he really was sorry, but I came to find out that his anger with his wife continually piled up and we were the recipients of when it boiled over.

My black eyes got darker. The bruises were more pronounced. My nose was crooked, but not fully broken, I don't think. It was a lot, too much, and it scared my friends from school when they did not see me there. We used to have a little corner store at the end of our street that had a payphone and I think one night I snuck out of the house, called my friends, and explained to them what happened. One of my friends ended up telling some teachers or counselors at the school the next day.

I think the problem for me was I went to their house after experiencing so much trauma prior to them. There wasn't any relief or support from the adoptive parents for the damage that had already been done. So, I was just expected to be this child, this daughter they never had. It was difficult. I would write really mean things. I used to love writing stories; little, short stories to get my feelings out. The mom would read those things, and her feelings would be hurt. In turn, she would lash out at me because her feelings were hurt too. The adoptive parents were very 'religious' people who went to church at least three days of the week. I eventually went to church when the bruises weren't as pronounced and they were healing, and I remember my mom buying all this makeup and putting it on me to cover up the bruises that were still visible. I remember feeling like everyone was staring at me like they knew something was wrong or different but were too scared to ask. My parents had fabricated some story about me getting into a fight at school. Now keep in mind I used to go to school all the time with bruises and stuff on me and then it came back that I was lying or I made it up, or oh, this happened, or oh, that happened. So allegedly this reputation was following me, but it was really hard to cover it all up. It's really hard to cover up a child's crooked nose and black eyes. So, they kept me out of school until I looked at least normal to try and prevent another social service visit, but they did not know I had already called my friends.

I eventually went to school. Social services had gotten involved; they asked questions. I don't remember what they did, but I just knew I was getting the fuck out from that house. I was like, "I do not want to go back to that house." And so I decided to run away, again. I waited a while and went to school for a couple weeks after the whole horrible incident. Then, my friends were going to some dance. It might have been a prom or something. This was my chance. Instead of going home that Friday, I went home with my friends.

As far as I can remember, I was probably 13 or 14, when I started running away a little bit. I guess I started bucking the system, is what I would say. I would run away because I really didn't enjoy being at their house. Like I said, it was very strict. I would run away and go stay at friends' houses and then I would come back. And sometimes they would come pick me up from some of these friends' houses. But it was mostly because I was tired of dealing with all the abuse and the lack of love. I didn't want to be there. I felt like no one understood me or cared. I felt like no one really wanted me there anyway. Just based on all the verbal and mental abuse I got from my adoptive mom as well as the physical abuse I got from my adoptive dad, I never felt like I was a part of their family.

I was in school, but I never fit in anywhere; growing up without any information on my biological family, not knowing who they were, and being in and out of other peoples' homes. It just automatically made me feel like an odd child, like I was always this black sheep. No one really accepted me. And it was like that with school and friends, I was never part of the IN crowd, and I dealt with a lot of jealousy and envy. And being that I never fit in, I didn't dress like everyone, didn't talk like everyone. My problems were totally different from my friends' problems.

Normally when I ran away, the parents would come get me by that night or the next day. Friday came and went. Saturday came and went. Sunday came and they still didn't come. So Monday, I went to school with my friends. When I ran away, I never ran away with clothes and shoes. I only had the clothes I had on my back, and the shoes I had on my feet. I would wear my friends' clothes and shoes. I would stay at my friend's grandmother's house and go to school because many of my friends all stayed with their grandmother. I stayed there, and then the guy I was dating lived not too far from where they lived, like a few blocks away. So, I would go over to his house and stay with him for a little bit, but I still went to school every day.

This went on, I don't know, maybe a week or two. And I remember this day like it was yesterday. I was always a straight A student. I excelled in school. I had no issues in school at all. In school I was in advanced placement classes. I absolutely loved school. It was an outlet for me. Reading books was an outlet for me as well. I thoroughly enjoyed interacting with my teachers, always longed to have a normal childhood, like the other kids. I was in ROTC, all four years. I played volleyball. I played a little soccer, ran a little cross country, played a little basketball here and there. So, I dabbled in sports and as much as I was allowed. I even participated in some clubs when I was able to. I loved the activities and stuff at school. I guess school was an escape from the things going on at home.

The adopted father allowed me to kind of spread my wings a little bit at least. Even though he was physically abusive, he was definitely there for me in some small and strange ways. I will never take that from him. Yet, it was a very, very painful and very strange relationship. Our mom would tell our dad if we did anything wrong and he would discipline us. Sometimes it would be a bit much. Ok, sometimes it was way beyond a bit much. Nevertheless, he was there for all my school activities and sports I played. He knew my friends. He chaperoned field trips. And he would talk to me for hours just about life and the do's and the don'ts from his experiences. He was just always trying to teach me things. These conversations would go on for hours and hours, and I felt like it was a form of punishment. But I later realized that was one of the ways he showed love. His outlet was instilling what he could in me, and I appreciate it to this day.

CHAPTER FIVE

....

The Road to Emancipation

Okay, so back to the day I remember so vividly. We're at school getting ready for lunch break. Just so happened that one of my friends was in the front office and they see my adopted dad come in. Word got around that my father was at the school and they were coming to take me home, but I didn't want to go. Dad's in the front office having a fit because he was ready for me to come home. The front office staff told my dad he would have to wait a bit until lunch period was over because all the principals were on lunch duty. So he decides to try to find me himself. He leaves the front office and starts walking the hallways looking into classroom windows. This was definitely a no-no so the school resource officer escorted my dad back to the front office. He then calls the mom; she comes up there. Now they're both arguing in the front office and she's like, "I told you not to come get her".

Word travelled to the lunch room that my dad was in the front office and he started walking the halls. My good friend, Kochera got a car; we snuck out of school and she took me to her grandmother's house, and I hid up in an attic just in case the police came. It was crazy.

I stayed at my friend's grandmother's house for a week or so. All the administrators and teachers knew what was going on so they did their best to support me. My schoolwork was being sent home for me to complete and my friends would turn it in for me. Then testing came up and I remember the principal asking me to call her. I ended up calling her and she was like, "Simone, I just have to tell you this. I can't get involved anymore because I will be aiding and abetting a runaway. I'm not able to send your schoolwork home to you. You know final testing is coming up. What I'm going to do is freeze your grades and whatever grades we freeze, that's what you're going to end this school year with. I'm going to give you this phone number to Child Protection Services (CPS). I've already reached out to them. They know your situation. I want you to call them and you have to work something out."

I reached out to Child Protection and they put me in contact with a lady named Barbara. She's communicating with my adoptive parents. She's communicating with me. A date and time was set for my parents and me to meet at the Child Protection office. They had already agreed to give up their parental rights. I was very adamant about not returning to their home. I made it to the Child Protection meeting and we're sitting up there and waiting for the parents to come. We waited for hours and we thought they weren't coming.

When they finally came, they showed up with the police. The police arrested me for being a runaway and for breaking and entering because I came back to their house and took my stuff that actually ended up being just fucking trash, but they arrested me anyway. I then was sent to the juvenile detention center and I was locked in this little juvenile cell for some hours, and the Child Protection lady, Barbara, did a petition for me to become, I don't know, I guess to be like a ward of the state again. Once that was filed I transitioned from the detention center to the juvenile shelter which was in the next building.

This is a lot for me, and keep in mind this is my junior year of high school. Yes, this is the way they treated their 'adopted' daughter, whom they wanted (at some point anyway). I put much of this at the feet of the parents who were constantly fighting about their own lives, and couldn't handle any 'stuff' from teenage children.

It's now the last day of school. I'm sitting in a juvenile detention center. Then I get remanded into the juvenile shelter and I don't know what the fuck is going on. I'm only 16 and I wasn't even old enough to go into this independent living program.

So I ended up spending my freakin summer in this juvenile shelter. I am sitting in this juvenile shelter experiencing every single miserable moment. I'm feeling like I'm incarcerated. You go to bed at a certain time, then you're locked in your room. You can't have stuff in your room or it would be considered contraband and you would be in trouble. It was an intense moment in life for me. I didn't know what was going to happen next. I'm sitting up here looking at these kids around me, like, I'm not as bad as they are. I just want to be loved. I just don't want to experience all the things that I'm experiencing. I just want to get out of this situation. Then I found out they have school there. But the school program they have inside the shelter does not count towards real school on the outside, so I wouldn't have been able to graduate on time. So my mission at this point is I just gotta get the hell out of this shelter so I can finish school, and on time.

CPS is working out something with the adoptive parents, so I can be emancipated from them because I said I never want to be back in their home again. And that was what I firmly stood behind. So my adoptive parents had a certain amount of days to come visit me at the shelter before they're charged with abandonment or something like that. So they came on the very last possible day to visit me. They came to visit me; I told them I was fine. I remember telling my brothers that I would miss them. The adopted mom said that I looked good and that I was finally getting what I wanted. I just shrugged my shoulders.

It was a really awkward visit to be honest. That day they gave up their rights to be my parents and the paperwork was completed for me to become emancipated, starting the summer of going into my senior year. You know, I'd never showed fear. I needed to be strong, so that's what I did but I really had no idea what was next for me.

My social worker at that time filed a petition to see if she could get me into an independent living program. This would allow me to finish school on time because she knew how important that was for me. It's very interesting to me how no one ever stressed school in my life, but I knew it was important to me as a way out. So I made it my business to do what I needed to do. I had to do a presentation to show I was mature enough to do the independent living program.

I ended up getting approved to go into the independent living program. Many of these independent living programs are privately run with government funding and some private funding. I went to a group home; that's how it is started. You'd go to a group home first, an all-girls group home. You have a big binder, like a manual that you have to go through and complete all the items in there, and it's stuff like how to use a fire extinguisher, or if you know how to iron, how to budget, how to pay bills, and you have to work. You had to have income, and you had to put away I want to say 70 or 80% of your check, and they covered all your other bills. They really covered all your bills in general, but they made it so you had to show them you knew how to pay bills with your own money, save your money, and then they would reimburse you. They would just do different things to prepare you to live on your own. That's really what it was. It wasn't long, I was prepared to live independently. No adoptive parents, no more whooping's, abuse, or disrespect. After spending my entire summer in a juvenile shelter, not knowing if I was going to make it out of there before my senior year was terrifying. I was excited for the next chapter of my life. A chance to make a way for myself.

To be an emancipated minor going into my senior year was wild. It was a moment that really didn't sink in until much later. I didn't have time to process my emotions then, but now, while I am writing this, everything is hitting me all at once. No biological parents. No foster parents. No adopted parents. I was really alone. So much coming at me at once. The all gas, no brakes was real for me then.

CHAPTER SIX

....

Independent Living

I was finally able to go into this girls group home, not too far from my school. This is right when school was getting ready to start for my senior year. I'm transitioning from one case manager to another inside this independent living program (ILP). I get my first job, so I'm working. It is all a bit confusing, for a kid having to navigate this new world and expectations, but I knew I had to persevere. Nobody in school really knows what's going on. They know I'm living on my own but they don't know all the details, but I'm just so focused on, I just gotta finish. It was a struggle. I worked. I went to school. Forget senior parties and festivities. I had no time for that.

In this group home they had a house parent who would come from like six o'clock in the evening till six o'clock in the morning. This was to prevent overnight guests. And that was also your time to work with the house parent to do your checklist from your manual. In order for you to graduate from the group home to your own independent living situation, you have to get everything signed off by the house parent and your case manager. There were so many moving pieces. I would do my little things with the house parent in the evening time, as my schedule allowed.

I would go up to my brothers' school, Michael and James and bring them little gifts, clothes, buy them something name brand, because those are the only brothers I really knew. When I was in the home, we were close, and we are still close to this day. I even connected with my adopted father. His constant apologies and me seeing him turn his life over to God allowed me to forgive him. Even though, yes, I did get emancipated from him, but he would come and visit me after school. Sometimes he would pick me up and we would have conversations. Very general talks, but it was nice to know that he still cared. The beginning of November, I successfully completed all the requirements of the group home. This meant I could transition into my own apartment! It was the week of Thanksgiving that I moved into my own apartment, my senior year of high school. Imagine that!!

It was a place called Appleton Apartment Homes. And it was a one bedroom, one bathroom apartment. ILP helped you get furniture; cosign on the apartment, they do all that. They also gave me a lump sum of money. The Independent Living Program (ILP) gave me about $1,000 to buy furniture and things I needed for my new place. This was truly a big moment for me in my life. I just remembered we got Thanksgiving off and it was my first weekend in my own apartment with me kind of decorating it and all. So, I know I'm giving just the very highlights of things in my life, and this was just one of them, but a very important one for me.

My apartment was between my first job at Dunkin Donuts, and Braum's Ice Cream and Dairy Shop, a restaurant, which I worked at both, not far from my school. I loved my little apartment and I still have a few pictures from that little one- bedroom apartment. I still had a case manager while I lived there, and they would just drop in sporadically. I wasn't allowed overnight guests still. You know, I still had to keep up with school and work, pay my bills and saving some, even though they really helped cover all the expenses. The whole goal of the ILP is to ensure you are able to take care of yourself and be a law abiding citizen. So, even though I had to pay bills, they would always reimburse me which I would then put into savings. Being that I was such a model kid in the program, they had me speak at events and programs for the state. I even received awards for being an exceptional child in the program from the Governor of Oklahoma.

I remember there were certain requirements in this ILP, so it was no walk in the park. I had to work, learn how to budget, pay my bills, go to school, deal with pop up visits. I didn't have time for friends… I was doing adult things very quickly. I am moving along through this program. I am working holidays. I didn't have much time for fun or even ordinary things. I successfully graduated high school on time, with honors. I was still dating the same guy, and his family was always there to support me even though his parents were divorced. A little chaotic, but they were there. They were supposed to come to my graduation, but something came up and graduation weekend festivities were very, very lonely and depressing.

I remember going to the 'baccalaureate' as they call it, on a Sunday. And it's the loneliest day in my freakin life. I was the only person in there representing me. And I can't remember if someone sang it or maybe played it, but it was the *Dear Mama* song by Tupac. It was 'mama, you know I love you.' And they were singing this song in support of parents and moms. You know being there for their children and getting to this point and it being a celebration. I didn't have a mom. And I never felt like I had a mother figure in my life. So even to this day, when I hear that song on the radio, I immediately turn it off. It just brings up too many negative memories.

I remember my graduation. I walked across the stage. A few people cheered for me, friends and their family members, and that was it. I remember going back to my own little apartment by myself. My boyfriend, at the time; I forgot he had some stuff going on. He was supposed to have been there, but he couldn't make it. We ended up going out to eat and that was it. I mean, prom was the same way. I mean, I could say I went, but it was hardly memorable and I just had too much stuff to focus on.

I was in ROTC for four years in high school and I absolutely loved it. Loved my instructors. I actually had joined the Army through the delayed entry program where you are joining the Army prior to your graduation from high school. Because that was all I knew, that was the only real positive example of a family unit I had. And I needed it. I needed something, so I joined the Army.

It was time for my lease to be up and I was ready to move from that place. I found this beautiful apartment that was a little further away, not on the side of town I was familiar with. I loved the apartment. It was like an old brick building that had individual units. It had bay windows. It was absolutely gorgeous. But I went into the Army and I couldn't stay there anymore, it made me so sad.

CHAPTER SEVEN

....

Brothers!

My brothers… Michael and James… they are the best brothers I could have had. As mentioned previously, Michael was adopted on the same date as I was. We all came from displaced homes, but grew up together in the same adoptive home. Michael and James are the same age; they're just a few months apart. They were just toddlers walking around when I arrived at the home.

Michael and I are both very fair skinned, so we used to get all the time that, "oh, we look like we're siblings, like we're blood." He's the father to three girls. These are my nieces. They were the only and first nieces that I've ever known. Having these brothers and family makes it feel like family… probably the best thing from my foster and adopted years, really, and the one thing I get to carry throughout my adult life.

Michael is the quiet and steady brother. Doesn't like to shake things up too much and very consistent. James is the flamboyant life of the party brother. A real jack of all trades guy and fun to be around. I was very protective of them. That was all I knew, even though we had other kids coming in and out of the house, those two boys were always there. We had our fights. We had our struggles growing up in our adoptive parents' home. We always thought James was their child, which was kind of implied by the adoptive parents; but I don't think they ever really said it directly to us. But James was adopted straight from the hospital, an infant as well, his name was changed, and he's a little darker skinned than we are. His skin tone was more of what our adoptive parents' skin tone was. It was always implied that he was their biological child and we were the foster kids.

James... the jack of all trades. He had no sense of time. Truly, going through life to the beat of his own drum, which no one else could hear. And James being James used to always be like, "oh, that's why your family didn't want you and you got to stay with my parents". Or "that's why you're here because your family didn't want you blah, blah, blah." So, we used to experience that all the time as kids but we didn't really take it personally, but sometimes we would. It would kind of poke at us a little bit. But today we laugh about it especially since we learned we were all adopted.

Those are the only brothers I've ever had. And they have always loved me and supported me unconditionally. In a very special way, that brotherly sisterly way. And to this day we are all very close. We spend many holidays together throughout the year. We talk several times a month, sometimes weekly, sometimes several times a week. Even when I was emancipated from our adoptive parents, I still saw them. I still reached out to them; I went to their school. When I went to the Army, I made it my business to say my goodbyes to them before I went to basic training.

Michael eventually went off into the Air Force and I would visit him. I was there for him and his wife at that time when they had their kids and still to this day, I spend a lot of time with my nieces. But I wanted to highlight my brothers because we all came from nothing; our common denominator was our adoptive parents. Which is another reason why I'm appreciative of my adoptive parents because they did take us in and that was a steep hill, but they took us in and the love and bond that we created; they played a part in it. And my brothers are the best thing to come from my adoptive situation. I don't know where I would be without them. They actually walked me down the aisle together when I got married! They have a relationship with my husband; my husband is an only child. So this is his first time experiencing brothers to this extent; just one more excellent thing to happen.

Even when I found my biological family, my brothers were right there, supporting me, embracing them as well. I mean, they just have always been there for me, even though they've never really known of all my struggles. They've always seen me as like this really strong, independent woman who has never given up. I'm like that rock for them. But truth be told, they have been a rock for me, and I know I could always call them. There were times where I wanted to quit life in general and just be a bum and lay on their couch, and they would have had no problems with it. Like, no matter who I am, what I'm doing. They've always accepted me and if they ever judge me, I have no clue what that looks like. At all. We laugh together, we cry together, we love on each other. And it's one of those things that everybody does the LOL which means laugh out loud, and but I always look at LOL as "Love out loud" because I felt like many times, I was loved in secret.

Especially after figuring out my biological family and the origins of how I came about in the path and life I took, but my brothers definitely love me out loud and they probably were the first expression of unconditional love I ever felt. So, yeah, those are my heartbeats.

I don't want to say we had an unstable upbringing once we were at our adopted home, but it looked very different. There were definitely challenges we faced, even though they might not have been able to connect the dots. But much comes from their origins, their biological family, from those genes and how they dealt with life.

I probably should share some very happy stories because, with them, although yes, we used to get our ass beat, we had some amazing moments together, which we still laugh about to this day. So sometimes when we get together, I mean sometimes we do laugh about our beatings and how scared we were; we can laugh about it now because I truly believe we have healed from that. It's no longer an area that brings us anxiety or negative emotions. It's now a place of, it's a part of our life experiences but we've overcome it.

We're better people today; we really don't hold it against our adoptive parents at all. Yes, they were very strict; we didn't have much freedom. When I say strict, I mean strict. Everything on TV was parentally controlled. So, most of the shows that many African American people grew up watching like Martin, Living Single, all those crazy shows, we didn't have a chance to really experience that. We watched family friendly shows, we watched cartoons. We played kid video games. We would have play time, and play time was usually sometime after breakfast, when most of the chores and homework was done and everything was kind of done in the house. We were then sent outside and we were locked outside. The only time we could come in the house was to come in for a lunch break or a bathroom break. Other than that, we drank water from the water hose and enjoyed playing in our backyard.

And then after lunch, we were sent right back outside and not just sent outside, but locked outside again, you could not get in the door. Unless you beat on a door and you were like, mama, I gotta go to the bathroom. Then they might unlock the door for us. Our adoptive father, built most of the stuff outside for us. We had a basketball hoop that was attached to a really tall tree; we had playground sets (some he built, some he bought), treehouses, volleyball net, etc. Just many fun things for us to play or build with.

I remember one time we made a seesaw. We put a big old cement block in the middle, then put a big old, long, two by four on there. Then we would jump on one side and put a toy or even a little small brick on one end. I remember one time jumping on one end, we had a little brick on the other end and the brick went up into the air, but then I couldn't see it because it was so bright and sunny. Even though I had stepped out of the way, I guess I still didn't move far enough, and the brick hit me in the head so I had a huge gash in the middle of my head. And the boys laughed, nonstop. It was something like we would see on Looney Tunes. I could not do my hair for weeks after the seesaw brick incident. Yet, that did not stop us from playing. We climbed trees, sat on the roof of the house, ate pecans from our pecan tree, sucked honey from honeysuckles that grew in our yard. We loved being outside which is probably why I love nature so much, to this day. I feel like I'm very free when I'm outside which is a natural thing. But for me, it was definitely peaceful. And so my brothers and I, we had many great experiences.

We had great Christmases at our adoptive family's home. Like people really thought we were rich. We thought we were taken care of; we just didn't have normal shit like other kids did. Like we didn't have a phone. We couldn't watch TV. We couldn't hang out at our friends' houses. We couldn't get into cars with our friends. It was very, very strict. And you know, such is life. I mean we turned out okay, I guess.

Growing up, I cooked a lot… I mean A LOT! But we always had good food. It was one of the rules that if our adopted mom wasn't home by a certain time, I had to already start taking food from the refrigerator and freezer and figuring out a meal with a meat, a veggie, a starch, and a bread at every single dinner. And for lunch, it was always like typical lunch foods, lunch meat, bologna sandwiches, noodles, hot dogs, and for breakfast, it was always typical breakfast foods. Now that I think about it, I wonder if my love for cooking came from this time.

We went on summer vacations with our parents too. So it wasn't like we didn't live; it was just a little more challenging because it wasn't my family. I had experienced a lot before I got to their house. I was new to them and they were new to me. It wasn't like we were born together. But, if you were to see my brothers and me today, you wouldn't know that because we love each other so much.

CHAPTER EIGHT

....

My North Star

One of the main thoughts that has stuck with me, even as a little kid, was 'I just got to make it through this'. I had already felt there was something bigger for me. I just had to get through this. It became my North Star.

My North Star… some people have one. It is that beacon of hope you carry around, particularly in dark days when things are not looking up, not looking bright, and not looking like these days will ever end. We look to our North Star hoping and wishing things will get better… today… tomorrow… or very soon! Not sure how or why or when, but we keep looking to our North Star with thoughts it will get better as long as we can see that Star.

And then another kind of North Star for me was, this… this life… is not my family. I need to find "MY" family. It was like I always felt I was lost and I never fit in, you know. It was like every home, every place I had gone to, I've never fit in, I wasn't really accepted, I wasn't treated well. And I was like, I just got to keep pushing through to get to whatever else is for me, and I just knew it would be something better. I had a purpose, you know, and this was NOT my purpose. This abuse I was experiencing, the different homes I was going through; just all the trauma. This is not what my purpose is in life.

And for some reason, I even knew that as a kid. There used to be a song that I would always sing. The song was called *Somewhere over the Rainbow*, from the movie, The Wizard of OZ.

That song used to bring me so much peace and comfort:

Somewhere over the rainbow
Way up high
There's a land that I heard of
Once in a lullaby

So when I was in the garage, laying on concrete floors, and trying to keep myself warm, I would sing that song in my head, just kind of rocking myself and it gave me peace:

Somewhere over the rainbow
Skies are blue
And the dreams that you dare to dream
Really do come true

I just knew I only had myself and I couldn't let myself down. I just had to make it through. And it's crazy because back then, especially in my adoptive family home, I used to overeat. I was very angry and I didn't understand all the things that were happening to me or why things were happening to me.

I used to write letters and different poems about how I hated my situation. How I hated this family. How I just wanted to get away from them. How I just wanted to run away:

Someday I'll wish upon a star
And wake up where the clouds are far behind me
Where troubles melt like lemon drops
Way above the chimney tops
That's where you'll find me

The foster and adopted parents saw these letters, and I don't know how far back those letters went; I don't know if I wrote them in other homes. But I do remember writing those letters. So, while writing was an outlet for me, reading books was an even bigger outlet for my feelings and desire for knowledge. And it's crazy because at my adoptive parents' home, one of my punishments anytime time I did something wrong or I was in trouble, they would actually take all my books away from me. Like I was one of those nerds; I loved to read and I would read any and every book I could get my hands on, and reading was an escape for me. It took me out of the present moment and took me to other faraway lands and experiences I knew I could have one day. I just had to make it through.

Somewhere over the rainbow
Bluebirds fly
Birds fly over the rainbow
Why then, oh, why can't I?

I just need to find my real mom and dad; I just need to find them. The thought never dawned on me why they gave me away. How did I end up in this place? What was the reason, what role did they play? I just felt like I had to find them and once I found them, I would be okay. For some reason I knew I would be okay once I found my family.

If happy little bluebirds fly
Beyond the rainbow
Why, oh why can't I?

Even when I was in school, I never fit in. I was always like the pretty and super smart girl. But I didn't fit in with the nerds and I didn't fit in with my friends. Everybody had family. Everybody seemed to have a sense of purpose. I never did. I just knew this; whatever space

I'm in, it's a very fluid and non-permanent situation. And I just got to get through it, you know? So, it was a struggle, and especially going from home to home; never really experiencing unconditional love. I used to write about unconditional love all the time. I knew that what I was currently going through was not unconditional love, and that was definitely something I desired. Something that I really pushed for was that I must find what unconditional love is, and that means finding my family, then that's what I'm gonna do. And that's why I always had to drive to look for them, hoping to find them.

Yes, it was very much like trudging through waist-deep snow during a white-out, not having a clue if or where you are going, but knowing you cannot stop, you cannot take a break, you cannot give up. If you walk long enough and hard enough, you will find yourself somewhere, wherever that somewhere is.

Yeah, and I hate to say this because I was a kid, so it was hard to really understand what my feelings were and why, but I just knew I had to survive. So that was my North Star. Imagine, as a kid, knowing you couldn't really be a kid, you only had to survive. You had to make it to whatever the next situation was. I didn't get to enjoy my childhood. I didn't get to watch all the kids shows and experience those things. I was always on a level of survival as a kid even though I was in homes that took care of me to a certain extent, even though there was abuse and mistreatment in those homes, but I just knew all I had was me. And that's kind of how I operate. Like with my adopted parents, even though they cared for me and took me in, which I am appreciative of now, I wasn't appreciative then, but it was one of those things where they actually took me in when they didn't have to, and when every other family and every other situation did not. It was like I was just kind of this 'play with a toy for a little bit to them'. Maybe when you want to interact with the toy again, you pick it back up, and that's it. Then when you're tired of a toy, you gave it away. That's really how I felt. But my adopted family, they didn't, they pushed through their issues, and drama. I'm grateful for that today.

What else kept me going? It's so crazy after meeting and connecting with my biological big sister and learning how different our paths were. We have a six year age difference. And you know, we all had our own experiences, we all had our own struggles, we all have our own different perspectives, and our own different vantage points. My big sister, even though she experienced a whole lot of trauma and turmoil with our biological mom, because she was at an age where she could remember living in an abandoned building in New York, in these crack houses and with different men who were abusive, and then eventually going into foster care. I did not have experience that trauma and turmoil with our mom.

Thankfully my sister found her forever home, and her forever home was really good. It was very positive. She had great support, she had love, she had all of those things. While I, on the other hand, went into the system at a young age, even though I was stolen or given up as a baby, then ended up with this weird couple, to foster home after foster home, it wasn't a good situation. It kept getting worse and I was unhappy.

What kept me going were the thoughts of my real family. I kept thinking if this was my real family, my blood family, my biological family, I would not be going through these things. I would not be experiencing this abuse. I would not be where I am. I would be happier. I would be loved. I would know what unconditional love means and I have no idea why, I just automatically assumed that. I mean, I truly believe that all my experiences thus far were so traumatic and so chaotic that anything has got to be better than this. Interestingly enough, even after going through all that, I've always still had love in my heart, and just a positive outlook on life because I never wanted to let myself get too down or too depressed. I felt like if I just kept pushing forward, you know getting to the next thing, I will be okay.

It's crazy because even though I'm talking about my feelings and emotions now, which I've gone through a lot of therapy as an adult, kind of processing my feelings, and even though I'm in my forties right now, it's one of those things where I am still this kid, this little girl still looking for love, the love and affection that a family is supposed to provide. Still longing for the love from a mother which was also a part of my north star.

Acceptance was another HUGE battle I faced. That's what kind of kept me going, but I think I might have been 37 or 38 when I finally figured out who my family was, what their names were, where they lived, and my origins. Some were accepting of me and some weren't. And still after spending my whole entire life looking for them, and then getting to that point, I was still dealing with rejection. Acceptance issues, not feeling loved, not feeling appreciated, not getting that unconditional love from the family I had been looking for. My entire life as a whole was even more traumatic than I had ever experienced individually. It was one of those things where I didn't know if I was gonna survive that, but that's another story.

But now it's like I'm finally like taking a beat, being still, and realizing I don't have to keep pushing. I don't have to keep doing things. I don't have to keep having goals and accomplishments and these major tasks I'm undertaking. My North Star and what kept me going was just getting out of that situation and just focusing on my family. And then I got to my family and I was like what the fuck? And that is a whole chapter or two or three, down the line. I mean, I honestly thought that my real life or my biological life can't be as bad as what I'm going through right now. And yeah, it took me like almost 35-40 years to figure out obviously God knew what He was doing when he did it!

You know, it's just unfortunate I had to go through the struggles I went through, but after going through all those struggles, and experiencing everything I did, and eventually finding my family... I think I may be good.

CHAPTER NINE

....

In The Army Now...

It was now past time for me to get serious focusing on my journey searching for my biological family. It primarily started when I left high school and I turned 18, I was able to get a copy of my adoption file and didn't know exactly what that meant, but I got a copy of it anyway. It was a very, very, very thick folder of documents. Now, keep in mind, I was only 18. I was getting ready to go into the Army after graduating high school. So I didn't really have much time to focus on this adoption file, but I read it from beginning to end, and I was just really clueless on what to do next.

Something I have not spoken on at all is that growing up in the foster care system, and later being adopted, and then getting emancipated from my adopted family, I never knew what my real name was. I never knew what my real birthday was. I never knew where I came from.

So, I have this adoption file and there is a lot of information in there. And like I said, a lot of stuff I didn't know what was what, or how to connect any dots; nothing made sense whatsoever. I didn't have time to focus as I was getting ready to go into the Army. I had my adoption file with me and it traveled with me everywhere I went, including to Fort Sill, Oklahoma, which is where I did my basic training. I remember wanting to run away from basic training and try to focus on this adoption file. I was even willing to hitchhike back because I was still somewhere in Oklahoma, but didn't know how far Fort Sill was from Oklahoma City, which is where I was raised in my adopted home. But, at that time, I was going to figure it out.

Mind over matter. I made it through basic training and It was the first time I felt my adopted family supported me; they actually came to my basic training graduation. I remember that. It took me writing many letters to them, but they did show up. I remember that day very vividly. I also remember the boyfriend I had at the time, before I went into the Army, who was the only boyfriend I really had in high school. He was there too and he proposed to me! It was my first proposal ever. I mean, of course, I was still only 18 years old.

After basic training, I went to what we called Advance Individual Training (AIT). I ended up getting stationed at Fort Belvoir, Virginia, to learn my job, my trade. I took my adoption file with me and I was, okay, I've got a little bit more freedom. So let me work on this. I would pick it up again, and read through it from beginning to end and still ask myself, "what in the world is all this information?" Nothing made sense? Who are these people? You know, where are they? I just didn't know what to do with the file, and I was separated very far away from my social workers I originally had. Because I was moving around with the Army, I wasn't able to reach out to them and ask for assistance, guidance, or direction. I really didn't have any assistance or anyone I could talk to because, when you're in the Army, you're going through one training session after another in different skills. It's very aggressive and the stress levels are 1000 % consuming. And it takes over your life, so I really didn't have, once again, the time to focus even in AIT. Afterwards, I moved to my permanent duty station, which was Fort Bragg, North Carolina. I was hoping for more time to commit to learning more about myself and my adoption file.

Originally, I was supposed to be stationed somewhere else in the army, but I asked for a transfer and traded locations with someone because, one, I wanted to be Airborne, which means I wanted to jump out of planes. Why? I have no idea! And two, I didn't want to be out of the country, and I believe they were trying to station me in Germany for my first duty station. I felt like I still had a lot to do with trying to find my family and I wouldn't be able to do that very well being in Germany. So I got transferred to Fort Bragg, North Carolina.

I got to Fort Bragg and let's just say life was definitely busy. I deployed overseas; I went to Kuwait and Iraq. I traveled the world. I was on the go and my little old adoption file just kind of sat in a cabinet in my room in the barracks, collecting dust. So the whole time I was in the military, I really could not focus on finding my family. I tried to keep up with my adopted... well, I guess you can call it my ex adoptive family... because I did get emancipated from them, and it was a very tough relationship that had its highs and its lows, which it probably always will.

I kept in contact with them, wrote them letters, and tried to visit with them whenever I could. Of course, I got to see my brothers when I could, just traveling to see them as they were kind of going through high school and things like that. And so it really wasn't until I transitioned out of the Army that I really picked up that adoption file. I started diving really deep into it. The Army afforded me the option to travel, so I had the travel bug in me; I was traveling all the time. But keep in mind I still never had a birth certificate. And back then you didn't really need passports and all these documents to move around like we do today. When I got out of the Army, I moved to Atlanta, Georgia. Now keep in mind, and I don't want to go into too many details with the military because some stuff is confidential or classified, but I had several deployments, of course. 9/11 was during my time in the military. As I mentioned above, I did deploy to Iraq and Kuwait in support of Operation Enduring Freedom, and Operation Iraqi Freedom, and was also caught up in the 'stop loss', which for those who are not military, that means when your particular job is in demand, whether you're supposed to get out or not, whether you're supposed to go off to a training or not, whether you're supposed to go to school or not, the military is going to keep you and you have no control over which way or where you go. So that happened to me. I love the Army. I love the family bonds I created, and it afforded me things I really didn't have growing up. I became part of an organization called the Prince Hall Masons and Eastern Stars while I was in the Army. I just had that sense of connection I never had as a kid. I didn't have that growing up at all. A sense of belonging, a sense of passion, a sense of I knowing what I was doing, and I enjoyed every moment of the Army. I am glad I made the decision to enlist.

When I was in the Army, there were many things I wanted to do that I wasn't able to do because, one, I was really good at my job and when a stop loss hit and 9/11 happened, I couldn't advance the way I wanted to in certain areas. I wanted to go off to West Point; I had put in packets and finally got things approved. But then the military, the particular division I was in, they needed me more, so I had to stay. So, I ended up deploying, I went to Iraq and ended up staying over for a good bit when I was supposed to be transitioning out of the military.

The reason I had made a decision to transition out of the military once my time was up, and I didn't renew my contracts, was because I wasn't maximizing my potential. I wanted to do so much, but the military just took priority. I was like, 'okay, I guess I'm gonna have to get out sooner than I had anticipated. And it's okay because I knew God had me covered'. So I ended up transitioning out of the military, but as I said, when I was supposed to transition, I deployed to Iraq. I came back from Iraq and they were like, okay, soldier, you got 30 days. So originally, I wanted to go to school, I wanted to study forensic science. I had plans on going to University of Central Florida, but because I only had 30 days to transition, I didn't have the time to get all my ducks in a row and get things acclimated and set up in a place where I had never lived, had never really been to, and wasn't familiar with. So that wasn't a good transition for me.

That is how I ended up in Atlanta, Georgia, because I used to drive there all the time, and many of my Masonic family were in Atlanta. I still had a sense of community by transitioning out of the

Army into the civilian world and by moving to Atlanta. This is the longest place I have ever lived in my entire life. I'm trying to get my feet underneath me to navigate the civilian world, how to pay bills, find a job, and finish college, things like that because I was in school a little bit here and there in the Army when I was able to take classes at night and on the weekends.

So, I want to say maybe 2007 or so, I decided to pick up my adoption file and I had some good friends and people around me who wanted to help, and everybody took a look at it. And when I tell you everybody, I mean they just threw their hands up; they were like, I have nothing. No one could do anything, or offer any support, any guidance. What about this? What about that? And something that was really irking with me was I couldn't travel as much as I wanted to because I didn't have a passport. I was able to travel in the military since I didn't need a passport. And I didn't have a passport because I didn't have a birth certificate. So that started my journey of trying to figure out how to acquire a birth certificate, which means I was very deep into this adoption file and trying to figure things out while communicating back in Oklahoma which is where my adoption officially took place. And going back and forth, I remember in 2008, I planned a trip to Oklahoma and God rest his soul, my good friend Jazz allowed me to stay with him as I was working with the court system that handled my adoption.

I wasn't certain if my trip back to Oklahoma City was successful. Then I came back to Georgia and submitted official documents, stuff with court seals, and things like that. I only had those original copies because, of course, the passport administration office would not accept just generic copies or Xerox copies. So, I had to send official documents and I wrote a letter saying, 'please, please, please, please, I pray that I get these documents back' and kind of outlined my story. I had been denied previously for passports and I remember I believe it was 2008, going into 2009 that I submitted all my documents. And in early 2009, I had an envelope from the Passport Administration, and it had my passport!!

I was like, this was such a MAJOR accomplishment, it was amazing!! During that same process of me focusing on getting my passport, I was buried in papers from the adoption file. I'm taking notes, I'm highlighting things, I'm asking people questions. What about this? What about that? I believe at this time I was employed at a particular job and I had some people there, some coworkers who were a little older, so they were a little bit more focused and had a bit more wisdom, and they offered me some guidance.

I had friends who were police officers and GBI agents working with the Missing and Exploited children's division who were just as lost as I was. I had friends all over and people would look at this adoption file and they just saw a big cluster fuck, like, excuse my language, but it was like… 'What in the entire world'? I couldn't blame them. I would give it to people and they would try to figure stuff out. Sometimes they got some new answers or just even just a new avenue, or a way to look at something, or maybe even another thing to research or search. But for the most part, it just took so much work. It was a lot for any one person to take on, or even just to understand it.

I felt so alone and isolated with my adoption file. I would pick up the file when I could. I remember where I was working at the time when some older associates would do their part and try to help me. I still have all the sticky notes and things they gave me to look into and they did what they could, and I'm super appreciative of it because man, if they had not done it, I don't know where I would be, even though I felt like I didn't get very far with the many different people who picked up my file and tried to assist me.

Sometimes it was just an inch, but just the motivation necessary to keep going, and then there were times I would get so discouraged I wouldn't pick it up for months. There were times I didn't even pick it up for years. But every little bit helped. And so, I remember being able to travel internationally for the first time in 2009 and I have not stopped traveling since. Any place I could go and explore, I was on top of it. I was using this passport as much as I could because it was something I never thought I would obtain. I took my first trip traveling internationally; I think I went to Jamaica, of all places.

CHAPTER TEN

....

The Journey of Searching

From 2009 until 2012 I hardly did any work on searching for my biological family, or should I say I was mostly busy travelling the world, but nothing of substance popped up anyway. I would pick up my file and skim through it, looking for that light bulb, to see if anything popped out that I might have missed, but nothing was coming to me.

In 2011, something strange happened during my search, or non-search you might call it. I don't even remember how I came across this family on my journey, but a father had lost his child in New York and they thought I was the missing daughter. The story really did line up... sitter was watching 'me' and then one day they took off with 'me' and never returned. The father said the mom was on drugs really badly. It happened in the Bronx. Timing was pretty exact. I spoke to the alleged father and then some other family members. They were so excited about connecting and finding their missing loved one. When they started sharing pictures that is where the doubt creeped in. I was like, "is this really me?" It didn't look like me, but how would I know?

So I asked about a DNA test. This was before I knew anything about DNA ancestry. I had identified a lab that specialized in paternity testing. I told the family how much it was and that would be the next step before I traveled to see them. We kept in contact for a while, they were trying to get the resources together to do the test. I'm so glad I held my ground and said I would only pay a portion of the cost. They never got the money together, so no test was done, but I had moved on from them and was able to rule out that family in a number of ways.

Then one day one of my Army girlfriends, Meaghan, called me yelling at me for coming to North Carolina and not telling her. I was so confused as I was not in North Carolina, well, not recently... and not in quite a while actually. She swears she saw me in a hair salon. We came to find out it was a girl who looked very similar to me, we could have been sisters. She was a younger version of me. So my girl Meaghan was telling me how she stopped this girl in the salon thinking it was me and started chatting with her. Her name was Jessica and she and her sister, Jasmine, lived in Gastonia, NC, just outside of Charlotte. So Meaghan tells them about me and a little of my story. She strongly believes there may be some family connection due to the very strong resemblance. Eventually the sisters and I connect and work out all the ways to see if we are related.

Jasmine is the eldest of the sisters and worked in the field of hospice care, so she had a little background in finding loved ones for those patients who were not going to make it much longer. Jasmine started down the rabbit hole of tracing her family background and eventually came up empty handed with no connections. But she continued to assist me with my own journey. I sent her a copy of my adoption records and she got to work. We tracked down some leads from my file and we were able to find out that Major Roberson was deceased. We went on to look for his death certificate because it would have valuable family information on it. We sent a request to the Iowa Vital Records office to obtain his death certificate.

Unfortunately, we could not get a copy sent via mail because I didn't have any legitimate documents that supported this man being my father, or that we were even related in some way. So that left us stumped. Then, one day, social media really worked out in our favor. I posted that I was looking for someone who lived in Iowa who could do me favor. A friend connected me to a Masonic brother whom I've never met. I spoke to him about needing someone to walk into the Vital Records Department and pick up a copy of the death certificate. See, death certificates are public record, and anyone could go in and get a copy. But to have it sent via mail or any other delivery option, it would have to be certified which requires much more paperwork. So the man I spoke to understood what I needed. And being that I also followed the Star in the East, he said he would circle back when he had some new information. Some time passed; I don't know how long... maybe months.

Then eventually I got an email from my Masonic brother with the death certificate! Just right there in my inbox! I could not believe it! Although he lived in Iowa, he was hours from the Vital Records. However, there was a young Masonic brother in college near the Vital Records. After several attempts, the young man was able to obtain the record and they scanned it to me. Incredible!

Now, the death record only gave us so much information that we had to research, which eventually led to some dead ends, but at least it was something. And this is how my search has always been... get a little bit, then I exhaust the research until it leads me nowhere. Just more information that either ruled out something, didn't make sense just yet, or it just wasn't valid to me.

Jasmine was a Godsend. She helped with as much as she could until she didn't know what else to do. Eventually, I met her and her sister in person one Thanksgiving (maybe 2013) as I spent the holiday visiting Meaghan, and we all had a good time. To this day, we are all still connected and we catch up with each other from time to time.

The journey continued as I somehow came across an article on a celebrity being reunited with her biological parents and using a company called Birth Parent Finders. It was a really nice story and it gave me hope after reaching so many dead ends. I reached out to Birth Parent Finders and sent an inquiry. This was also the year I was first introduced to DNA ancestry. Initially, Birth Parent Finders did not want to take me on. My case was 'too difficult and not enough leads to go on.' This was very disheartening. It also let me know all the work I've put in thus far, there is a reason why I haven't gotten anywhere. I felt extremely defeated. I had written to Oprah numerous times, and the Maury Povich show, and so many more, to try and get someone to help me. Nothing.

Eventually I picked myself up again and did the DNA ancestry kit in May of 2017. Even with those results, the closest relative was a fifth or sixth cousin and no one knew what to do about it. I hired Diana with Birth Parent Finder and she did what she could with my DNA ancestry results which ruled out many things. One thing Diana did was connect me to Toni Roberson who was Major Roberson's daughter, who was also mentioned many times in my adoption file.

Diana connects with Toni and tells her that she's working for someone trying to get information on her biological parents. She shares with Toni pieces of my adoption file that confirms this information is legit. Without question, Toni does acknowledge and confirms Major Roberson is her father.

So I connected with her and asked her to do a DNA test. Now keep in mind, I live in Atlanta, Georgia. What are the odds that Toni lives in Georgia, as we were communicating? This woman lived in Hinesville, Georgia. She's disabled and has a son who is disabled and lives with her. They are both on a fixed income. I ordered her a DNA kit from the DNA ancestries website. I get it and I send it to her, telling her what she needs to do. I really tried not to push her. So, it took a couple of weeks before she finally did it, and sent it off. And, from that day on we pretty much talked daily, because we thought we could be sisters, and it was just an interesting situation. She didn't know me at all and I didn't know her. She didn't believe her father could have fathered a child after her because the accident that injured him happened when she thought she was about 10 or 11. And we're about 12 years apart right now. So that means he would have already been injured when I was allegedly born. But she did know Betty Roberson;

she had met the lady a couple times, and she did not care for that lady, didn't care for her at all. So, as we're waiting for the results to come back, I had promised I would come out and meet her, her and her son, so I did. The results had come back and confirmed that her father was not my father.

It confirmed that she's not my sister. And that's what it is. I am very disappointed this is another dead end road on this journey. But there was a little glimmer of light in this situation. Being that I used DNA ancestry as the DNA collection tool, it connected her to family members that she had not been in contact with in a long time. They knew of her, she knew of them, but that was it. So, it ended up connecting her to two particular people who were her father's sisters, which would make them her aunts. They immediately welcomed her and they have been in contact ever since. I've helped her with some assistance with her disability, and I mean, it's a beautiful story. There's just so many pathways off this story that got me to where I am today.

Toni ends up telling her Auntie Paula and Auntie Wendy the story about me and they immediately want to talk to me. At the time, I'm a little down. I'm a little depressed and disappointed the results weren't favorable, and didn't link to anything for me. Or at least I thought... So, what ends up happening? Toni reaches out to me, and she's like, "my Aunties want to talk to you, here's their information, give them a call."

I said, "okay, I will". It took me some weeks to finally give them a call; I wasn't in any rush. I don't know why they wanted to talk to me, even though I think Toni did say she thinks they might have some information that might be able to help me. But I was kind of bummed. I eventually called them, and we talked, we're exchanging pictures, Facebook, you know, connections and stuff, social media handles, and they explained to me how they met Major, and how he was their brother, but they had different fathers.

The sisters, Paula and Wendy, were telling me that Betty and Major came to visit them in the Bronx for some time and it was just the two of them. Eventually, they kind of disappeared for a little bit, meaning they had left their house and had been gone for some days, weeks, months. And their oldest brother, who they were kind of raised with and also lived in New York, had told them they had seen Betty's van around the neighborhood, around the Bronx. It's a very distinctive van, especially with it being wheelchair accessible. So, he was saying, "I've seen their vehicle around".

"So, when they reappeared back at their house, they had a little girl with them. They told them it was a little mixed girl, that the little girl definitely looked like she could have been mixed with white and black. So okay, so what ended up happening? Where'd you get this little girl? Where have y'all been?"

"My Aunties," Paula and Wendy, told me that all kinds of stories about where they got you were floating around. They said they had gone to the Long Island area, and they had adopted you, or were watching you for somebody or something like that. But they were young themselves, they didn't feel like the story was true, and they knew Betty was a liar. But they just let it ride. They did not have the means to explore the truth about it. So, Paula and Wendy are sharing what they remembered about this little girl, who they do believe was me. I was very quiet, very withdrawn, and would attempt to play with all the other kids. I was still in diapers at the time, but they remember me transitioning out of diapers into panties. They remember Betty going to the store with them pulling out a wad of cash and buying me probably like 100 pairs of panties, is what they said, their words not mine. "Betty always took care of you guys", she said, you guys meaning Major and me.

Eventually, Betty and Major and this little girl, which allegedly was me, end up leaving, never to see them again. Never to hear from them again, and Major ends up dying shortly after.

I start connecting the dots from my adoption file. I was born allegedly in 1982 and was attacked by the dog in 1984. So, the story is definitely aligning. That means I was only two years old when I was attacked by the dog. And, gosh, it's just crazy how these pieces are fitting into this puzzle.

I believe Major's death record says he passed away in 1985, maybe in November. I entered foster care in 1986. So, for a little bit of time, it was just me and Betty out on the road, going from state to state. My adoption file shows us going to Missouri, Kansas, and Oklahoma, where I entered foster care, technically.

CHAPTER ELEVEN

Pieces of My Puzzle

So those DNA Ancestry results sat on a shelf collecting dust until one day I was chatting with a friend and they recommended I reach out to the National Center of Missing & Exploited Children (NCMEC) Division. In 2018, I submitted a request through NCMEC to see if they would take on my case. With my case being so unusual they decided to take it. Now keep in mind, they get requests daily and only take on a few. I was assigned a coordinator, Brenda, and she was helpful. She connected me to the Atlanta Police Department (APD) Missing Unit where I met with Detective Tia, who scheduled me to come in to collect my blood and DNA samples to submit in the missing CODIS database. At that time, all the different DNA databases did not speak to each other and were protected. I know times have definitely changed, but this was the reason why the Atlanta Police Department (APD) had to collect my DNA even though it was in the DNA ancestry already.

After having my DNA collected by APD and waiting on the results to come into NCMEC so they could compare to what they had in their database, Brenda suggested I connect with a Facebook group called DNA Detectives. I immediately joined the group and was blown away by all the individuals who were searching for family members! All this time, I thought I was on an island, all alone and no one could understand my plight. I got wrapped up in reading all the stories and requests until I decided to jump out there with my own request.

I posted what I was looking for, refined it a bit here and there as I learned the process. So, in this group, you can request assistance by way of a 'search angel.' They review your DNA information and start tracing your family. Some people are more advanced than others. There is no charge and no exchange of money. They do it out of the kindness of their hearts and the passion for this type of detective work. So I made my first post and got nowhere. I sat on it for a month and made another post. In that month, I was watching, reading, and researching what others were doing in the group and trying to apply it to my own journey. I did not get very far, so I made another post, specifically asking for a search angel. This was in November of 2018. Lots of people commented and asked questions to get the juices flowing, but most was not helpful information. Not until I got my very last comment on my Facebook post from Virginia Thompson, and my journey of searching exploded.

CHAPTER TWELVE

....

Search Angel

Virginia Thompson sent me a private message on Facebook telling me not to be discouraged, and she would work on my case. She sent her mobile number and told me to call her when I got a chance. This was in November of 2018. We have been joined at the hip ever since! She listened to my story, became a collaborator on my DNA ancestry account, and we were off and running. I sent her a copy of my complete adoption file as well.

Virginia loves this work. She is a retired school teacher from Tennessee. She pretty much taught herself how to trace family, using DNA matches, genealogy research, and just grassroots detective work. She started with connecting the dots with her own family and then started helping others, which allowed her to learn even more.

We exchanged email addresses and Virginia went to work with what she had access to. I remember her telling me I needed to do '23 and Me' and I was like, REALLY?! I was so frustrated with spending money and dead ends that I had lost hope. But Virginia brought hope back. Unbeknownst to me, she was exactly like what have I gotten myself into! My project was hard. Others before her told me this and I had experienced so many challenges on this journey, so I did not expect much.

Yet, Virginia never gave up. She is a night owl, retired woman who did her best work in the wee hours of the morning. I would wake up to 4-6 emails from her just working away.

In February of 2019, I remember being in Colorado skiing with friends. I took her call after getting in from the slopes. She told me that she identified my paternal side of the family, but wasn't sure who was who. Now keep in mind, these DNA databases update nonstop as more and more people became interested in pursuing them. So she was tracing family trees from 4th and 5th cousins and working backwards! Hard work, but she stayed at it.

Of course, she was excited to share the news and it took my emotions into overdrive. She explained how she had reached this outcome and how she had sent certified letters to two guys and was waiting to hear back. She found their social media page and I asked her to send it to me. In my mind I was thinking they may be wondering who is the white lady, but they might be more open to responding back to me. The other Facebook account was not as active from what we could tell. However, both accounts were Clarence Cross, but two totally different people... but they were connected.

So, while I was in Colorado, my last few days there, I sent a private message to one of the guys who looked like he was closer in age to me and said, "What's up?" The day I flew back home I got a response back, "What's up?" from Clarence Cross. My heart was beating so fast. I got home and got in my car, I was going to grab food and then pick up my dog from the sitter. While I was sitting and eating, Clarence and I were messaging back and forth. I asked him if he knew who I was. He said, "yeah, I know who you are!" Now keep in mind that I was messaging him from a space that I know he may think I'm trying to 'holla' (slang for trying to pick him up) at him, when really I'm just trying to see how we are related. Also keep in mind that Virginia had traced so much information that linked us, so I knew a ton of stuff about him and his family, but still didn't know the exact relationship. So when he said he knew who I was, I flipped out and told him to call me and sent my number to him!

He called me and I told him briefly my story and that I was sorry to bust his bubble that I'm not trying to date him, but that we are related some way. He was very excited and helpful. Even said he wouldn't be surprised that his dad could be my dad as well! I got Virginia on a three way call with us and she explained even more details that I wasn't clear on and Clarence confirmed much of it. Wow!

So the very next step was to take the DNA test... he agreed and we met for the first time less than a week later. He lived with his mom 20 minutes from me! How crazy is that?! The universe!

When he first saw me, he was like, "you look just like my pops." It was wild! We sat on his porch and agreed to not say anything to his mom about who I was until we had confirmation back. So I met her, but she thought I was just a friend. Even she was looking at me like I was familiar.

He asked me to set everything up with the account with DNA ancestry. He spit in the tube, we sealed it, and I mailed it off the same day. Clarence (also known as Clay) and I talked every day, and for hours some days. We had grown close.

On March 17, 2019, the results came back at like two something in the morning and of course Virginia was up. She called me and said, "HE'S YOUR BROTHER, SIMONE!"

CHAPTER THIRTEEN

New Brother on The Block

S o, the results from the DNA ancestry came back in March of 2019; it just so happened to have been St. Patty's Day. I remember exactly where I was because I was staying at a friend's house. My house was being rented out for an Airbnb when I had just gotten back into town. I was also planning to hang out with my best friend later that day to celebrate St. Patty's Day, because I do have about 4% Irish in me (thanks to DNA ancestry for this information). I remember waking up everybody at my friend's house, and just crying and just being so excited and overwhelmed with emotions.

Later that day, I spoke to Clarence, my brother, and told him the results came back and they were showing him as my brother. He was so excited. He started spreading the news around to family and the other siblings who are additionally two other sisters, an older and a younger, and then he told our father that he has another child out there and man there was a lot, I mean, a lot of emotions going on. From what I remember, I felt like I spoke to everyone that day including my father, but he wasn't excited. But that is not surprising.

And of course, I think many people were very cautious because they didn't know what my intentions were. However, I didn't have any intentions. I was just looking for my family, and I had been an open book, and kind of like, here I am. I found you guys, I'm so happy, and coming from the space of, I had such a rough life growing up that I always knew if I just found my family everything would be alright. But needless to say, everything was not alright. I remember when I first spoke to my dad and kind of explaining the process, he really wasn't under understanding what I was saying. Or at least he made it seem like he wasn't understanding.

Then I ended up getting Virginia, my search angel, on the phone because she's a little older. You know, closer in age with him, and may be able to explain things a little bit better to him than I can because she's a more knowledgeable of how everything breaks down. So she explained things to him, and he still wasn't very receptive to me. He was just like, "Let's not get ahead of ourselves. It looks like you've done a lot of work. Now we need to figure out who your mom is," because at the time I did not know who my mom was, or her name, or what the maternal side of my family looked like at this point.

Now when I think about it, I think he was also just kind of being cautious; he knew there was another child out there. I felt he was just kind of speaking very cautiously and kind of putting it out there that no one ever told him he had another child somewhere. So I just kind of accepted what he said at that time, at that moment, because I had nothing else to go on. But it was a little abrupt for me.

You know, my first conversation with my dad, and not really being fully accepted was disheartening. I was crushed; I cried. I didn't know what to do. It definitely deflated me like I had no energy. I had a flight the day after I spoke to him, and I missed my flight because I was just so distraught and in tears, and just didn't know why I was being treated this way.

So I eventually picked myself up, and brother Clarence has completely been supportive. He was like, I don't care what my dad says. I remember Clarence was like, "I used to have dreams about somebody being out there for me and I thought it was maybe a girlfriend, but I really believe that it was you, my sister". We built a really strong bond and I love him to death. We still keep in contact to this day on a regular basis.

You know it was in March I spoke to my dad and he would speak to me here and there. But after that first conversation, I just kind of fell back, and then the sisters… As I said before, there was an older sister and a younger sister who weren't very accepting either. Then I came to find out my brother Clarence and I are the same age, which also means that our father had two women pregnant at the same damn time. Clarence actually lives with his mom. So, it was a lot going on, you know? The skeletons in the closet were overflowing out of the closet at this point. Even though my brother's mom was divorced from my father, and he had since remarried and divorced again, they had a relationship because of the kids and grandkids they share; it definitely impacted her, you know? It impacted her in a way because she didn't know he had another child out there and she was pregnant at the same time as my mom was pregnant.

It hurt her feelings. At first, she was accepting of me; then she wasn't accepting of me. But now we're in a good space. So, it was a lot, and then the sisters, especially the younger sister, Charmaine, doesn't want to have anything to do with me. She says one thing, but does another. And it's more so, you know, she's a daddy's girl? And that's fine. As I said, I've never wanted anything from them but conversations and acceptance, and I had to learn they can't do either of those.

I realized a bit later, that allegedly, my father has money, and has always had money, and has taken care of his other kids and other family's kids as well. And there was a discussion on if I wanted money or back child support and all this and that, and I was just like, really? You know, they just started making up stories, not really knowing who I am and what I'm about, or even caring to know.

You know, they just wanted to build up whatever false thoughts they wanted to make of me. That's what they did. And that was hurtful. It is March going into April, I took a break from trying to figure out my mom's side of the family because the dad's side was just so heavy. And very chaotic, and it's still to this day; it's still that, but I'm definitely able to manage a little bit more of my father's side of the family.

Now fast forward to May, it was getting close to the end of May. I had told Virginia; I wasn't going to put things on pause for too long. So let's get back into working on my maternal side and trying to figure out those pieces of the puzzle.

CHAPTER FOURTEEN

....

My Sperm Donor, My Biological Father

As mentioned previously, my father would speak to me from time to time. March, April, May, June, July of 2019. We would have small conversations. I had to learn what to talk to him about that would not get me upset and keep him talking. He was a bit open to me and somewhat 'claimed' me, but he would never go into any details, as he stood behind the fact that no one told him he had another child out there, and that he never knew a Wanda Joyce Jones. Keep in mind this man was almost 80 years old.

Some things that I have learned about my father... some may be true, some could be just gossip. One thing I do know, is that the Cross-family name alone carried a lot of weight. My biological father, aka sperm donor, was a drug king pin in New York. People in all five boroughs knew the Cross's and STILL know the name Cross to this day. He sold drugs AND he worked in corporate America in New York. His corporate job: he drove for the New York transportation system for over 20 years and then for the school system as a bus driver for maybe another 10 years. He knew how to work the system and schooled others on how to do so, all while pumping drugs into others. He was friends with Nicky Barnes and ran in circles with that crew. If you know anything about Nicky Barnes and the drug world then you know it was 'Big' drugs.

He was known to frequent the Playboy mansion out in California as well. Come to find out, many of the Cross men had sex addictions that plagued the family and unfortunately, my father still feeds his addiction to this day. I truly believe that drugs and his addiction to sex is how his path crossed with my biological mother. He was a ladies man and the women loved him, and apparently, they still do.

My sperm donor also served a short stint (I served longer), in the Army as a cook, which he told me himself. Interestingly enough, my sperm donor and I share many similarities even though I was not raised by him at all. Of all his children (that we are aware of), I am the one who followed a path most closely to his. With going into the Army, handling business the way we do, and having a no-nonsense mentality, we definitely share those traits.

People loved and respected my sperm donor near and far. He took care of people and their kids. He provided for families in and around his neighborhood and still, to this day. He was very affluent for a black man raising a family in New York back in the day, and still to this day as a retired man trying to live out his years now with property in several states and countries. He made wise business decisions that really set him up. But unfortunately, he did not make the best decisions as it related to keeping his penis to himself and staying away from the 'young' women. He married and divorced four times.

So, our small conversations continued and I was really trying to keep a connection with him. Especially after finding my biological mom's family at the end of May. There were several key things my father would say that did not add up or did eventually add up. For example, when I was attacked by the dog. I was not familiar with the area, but later was able to connect the dots that the motel was in the Long Island region. This is where my father raised his family. Even

Major's sister once said that her brother and Betty told her they got me from Long Island.

Another dot that is loosely connected… one day I asked my brother Clarence, who named him and his younger sister since both names started with the letter C? He specifically stated our father named us; point blank, period. Funny, my birth name starts with a C, Calissa, and I will provide some more information about that in a later chapter.

This is just one of the many reasons why I want to talk to my father. Somehow a birth certificate is non-existent. His name could be on it. He knows way more than he is willing to share. His time is very limited and I feel like I will never get the answers I deserve.

CHAPTER FIFTEEN

························

Epic Fail

It's Friday, July 19. I drove up from Atlanta to North Carolina, and it was, I don't want to say, a random thing, but it was very spur of the moment. I was like, I gotta make an effort to try and meet him, because he's not going to. And the clock is ticking. Neither of us are getting any younger. So, I drove. After getting up at 5am, working out, working all day at the office, I got on the road, and drove straight to North Carolina.

My whole purpose, my sole focus, is to finally meet the man who contributed to my birth. I want to see him face to face. I want to talk to him. I think he knows more than what he has shared with me. And what he knows, he hasn't told anyone. So my hope is that when and if I meet him face to face, he tells me what happened. How did I end up with this man in a wheelchair and this white lady, to eventually land in foster care? What did he know about my mom? What was their relationship like?

When I arrived in North Carolina, and settled into my hotel, I called him. I was very, very nervous. I did document the call with an Android recording. I was praying he didn't answer the phone; that I would be able to leave a voice message. But he did actually answer.

It's not like I've never spoken to him before. It's not like he's never answered or returned my calls. But those calls were very short. Not the friendliest. Not the most warming conversations. Devoid of emotion, and more importantly, devoid of information. But last night wasn't so bad. It was only a 10 minute and 11 second call. Yes, that's how important it was to me. He answered; I told him I was in Charlotte, that I was here on business, which unfortunately was a lie, but I didn't want him to feel like I was some crazy stalker. But my sole purpose was to see him; and I told him I would adjust my schedule accordingly.

He didn't say he wouldn't meet with me, but he didn't say he was going to meet with me either. He said he would call me back within that day, and let me know his availability. Allegedly, he's not ever busy. Once I told him I was here, now, he's busy. He is around 80 years old… what the hell could be making him so busy, was running through my mind? So go figure, I'm sure he's probably thinking many things, which is why I didn't tell him in advance about me coming. I didn't tell any of our mutual family members I was coming because I didn't want it to get back to him. I didn't want him to think about it. I didn't want to ask his permission. I didn't want him to back out. So I just showed up.

I plan to stay till Sunday, and we'll see how it goes. I had arrived in Charlotte on Thursday evening, spoke to him and now it is Friday; no call from him yet. I was trying to be patient until at least the end of the day to try and give him some time to get back to me. I have a Plan B to call Uncle Vito. Uncle Vito is not my real uncle, but he's my brother's uncle, who is my father's son by a different mom. Got that? They get much more difficult as we get to know more family members. I have it all written down and even that doesn't help. Uncle Vito lives here in Charlotte and he and my father are very close, despite him being divorced from Vito's sister. At that time I had not met Uncle Vito; he seems to be an advocate for the truth which is what I am seeking.

So, I decided to reach out to Uncle Vito, if I hadn't heard from my father by the end of the day. I am hoping that once Uncle Vito knows I am here, maybe he will be a mediator, in bringing my father to the table to meet me.

I don't know what the outcome is going to be. However, I do feel Uncle Vito will make an attempt to do what he can. At this point, all I have is Saturday. My plan is to be out of here first thing Sunday, so I can get back to my life. So many thoughts were running through my head… And next steps? I'm moving forward with this whole situation; I have never experienced anything like this before. I don't know how to feel. I don't know what to feel. All I know is this journey has been heavy. I'm definitely just exhausted from everything, just mentally, emotionally, totally 100% exhausted.

It's just really pushing me to my limits. Sometimes I don't feel like I can handle it. I haven't really been in any life situation too many times where I couldn't handle it. And I've been in many crazy situations. I mean, I know what I want to happen. But it's obvious we don't always get what we want.

What I really want is, to talk to my father and to meet him face to face. How difficult can that be?

I feel like he knows my mom. He knows about her. He knows I know that he knows. He knew about me when I was a baby. I know a lot of things. A lot of things I'm sure my father didn't think I probably would ever find out; probably things he thought he would never have to face ever again. When I do speak to him, he always says he's living a good life. And to be honest, I don't really fucking care about his fucking life. I've had a fucking rough life. I don't wish death upon anyone. But I hope it's beaten him in the back right now. I really do. I hope he's having to face whatever decisions that he did or didn't do. I hope he's facing them, and that he is held accountable for his actions.

Even after all the shit I've gone through. I don't hold anything against my parents. I want a relationship with my biological family. Just as well as I want a relationship with my father. Of course, only if he is willing to be honest, put everything on the table, and tell the truth. I don't have time or energy for lies.

Now, what I would like to know... that I feel like I am entitled to know about 'ME'. I feel like I'm entitled to something. Like the who, what, when, where, and why. And not to judge, not to point a finger, not to incriminate anyone, not to make anyone feel bad. Not for any of those reasons, but primarily just to know where the fuck I came from.

Today, I know my name is Simone Danielle Bailey. I do understand and recognize my life for many of the things that I do now. However, my name before Simone Danielle Bailey was Calissa Cross and there's just so many unknowns and so many whys that I don't have answers to from that life. But it is a part of me, and I have never felt complete. I am a successful Black woman and yet, I don't feel complete.

Although, I feel like I'm really close to closing that circle, but it's not closed all the way yet. But I'm close and that's why I want to meet my father. That's why I want to know. That's why I want to find my mom. That's why I want to know my birth date. I want to know. IS it really that hard? I do wonder why my sperm donor won't part with this information? Secrets? Hardly. Embarrassed, 40 years too late for that. Worried I want money or something else? I have made that clear... he has nothing but information and answers for me. His money and worldly goods are his and I don't want one dime NOW. 35 years ago, maybe it would have been nice to get a Christmas gift or birthday card, but NOW, I don't give a damn. Just answers... and they are free.

I will see how this goes. I don't know how I'm gonna feel after this. I'm anxious. Lots of anxiety. Lots of which is sitting on the edge. Lots of questions swirling around in my brain. It's just a crazy situation to be in. And what if he refuses? I don't know, but I have to keep living without him and live my life. Maybe he will come back around in a week or a year or in ten years... but I won't give up til he stops breathing.

So, anyway, my father never calls me back. I speak to Uncle Vito and he invites me over to his house Saturday. My emotions are all over the place but I go to visit Uncle Vito and his wife. It's the same looks I have been getting from all of my dad's family and -ex-wife's family is that I look just like him. Out of all his children I resemble him the most.

Uncle Vito shares his thoughts on the situation. He feels like I've done everything I could except just popping up at my father's house. I then told myself I'm going over there as soon as I leave here…and I did. Uncle Vito did call my father and he told him he had a friend come into town (so he was tied up.) Like, really, dude?!?

I thank Uncle Vito and his wife and depart his house to head straight to my father's house. I am nervous as shit. I park at the curb. The neighbors on both sides of my father's house are watching me… intensely! I get out and knock on the door then ring the doorbell. No answer.

I don't know how long I was out there, a good 30 minutes or so at the front door, maybe longer, maybe not. I was distraught. What now? Neighbors are watching me. He is not answering. So I eventually get back in my car to try and figure out what to do next.

I eventually get out of the car again and go to one of the neighbors' houses and speak to them. I asked if they had seen my father recently. This man is staring at me like I look familiar. I tell him I am Clarence's daughter. I told him I was going to be in town, but he is not answering.

This man proceeds to walk to my father's garage and punch in a code, which lets the garage door open. I immediately freak out and yelled, "Wait, we can't do this." The neighbor tells me he watches his house and collects his mail when my father is travelling, so he said it was ok.

"He only has one car so if it is in the garage then he should be home." I felt like the garage door was moving so slowly, but eventually revealed a car. The neighbor said, "he is in there. Did you try knocking on the back door? He does have bad hearing." I told Jerome (the neighbor) that I wasn't going to the back, but I would try the front again. So we both went to the front porch and knocked really hard while ringing the heck out of the doorbell. Still no answer.

So I left Jerome with a message to give my father and whoever else he wanted to share it with. I had heard how private my father liked to be, so I told Jerome to let my father know his daughter who he attempted to give up, came by and I don't appreciate him leaving me hanging yet once again.

I went back to my hotel and cried my eyes out. Then I rattled off a slew of messages to my father via WhatsApp. Pretty much telling him he was a coward. I know he knew my mom and what he did to her. I let it out and finally got some rest so I could drive back home the next day. It was a very much wasted trip, but I can at least say I did all that was in my power to make the meeting happen.

It's Sunday. I've checked out and I'm on the road home. At some point on my drive my father calls me. I immediately pull out my tape recorder and press record. He starts off with a few words about how his weekend got busy; how he was riding with a friend in town so he really wasn't home... blah, blah, blah. I didn't believe a word he said. He then proceeded to tell me he would come to Georgia, and do a DNA test, so we could move forward. He said he would come next month, which would have been August. He went on to ask me about my mother since, in my messages to him the night before, I revealed that I had found them; that they knew him, and he was a liar.

I could tell he was shocked. He started stumbling over his words and wondering how they knew him. In a 15 minute call he repeatedly asked me if my mom was still alive or 'existing.' I told him she was at least 15 years younger than you, why wouldn't she be alive? Why do you keep asking me the same thing?

He never really answered any of my questions fully. But what I was left with after this call was that he knew more than he let on and now he is scared. That was the last conversation I had with him. He never came to Georgia in August or any other time to meet me. He has not answered a single phone call, text, or letter I have sent him. Just radio silent.

....

CHAPTER SIXTEEN

Did My Sperm Donor Name Me?

Another potential piece of the puzzle, my name, Calissa. My grandfather's name is Clarence Cross. He is the OG. My father's name is Clarence Cross; he is the second. And my brother's name is Clarence Cross; he is the third. My sister from the same father, younger sister, her name is Charmaine Cross. These are all CC initials, right?

So it wasn't until May 21, 2019, on this date, after all this time... that I heard someone call me by my BIRTH name. When I picked up the phone on May 21st at approximately three in the afternoon, and called my Aunt Marilyn, who is my mom's sister.

I called her and I said, "Is this Marilyn?" And she says, "yeah, this is Marilyn." And I said, "Hi, I'm Simone." This woman I have never known; she's never seen my adoption file. But my name in my adoption file is Calissa. But I wasn't really sure if it was really my name, or the name that Betty and Major Roberson gave to me.

A side note: there was talk that Betty and Major could have stolen me from my mom or from a 'sitter.' My mom would leave my oldest sister and me with. That could very well be true. I was told my mom was an addict, that she was not mentally stable. She could have been tricked or something. My oldest sister on my mom's side definitely remembers going back to the 'babysitter's house' and I was no longer there. But anyhow, back to Aunt Marilyn.

So my Aunt Marilyn, as soon as I say 'Hi, I'm Simone,' she kind of yells out in excitement as she says, "Calissa, it is so good to hear from you! We have been looking all over for you. I'm so glad to hear your voice!" So, she's just constantly saying my name and when I heard her say Calissa, I knew the shit was real. I knew this was my family! She wouldn't have known this at all, in any shape or form. The only way she would know my name is if this woman really knew me! So, I literally break down in uncontrollable tears because I'm like, 'Oh, this piece of the puzzle which is HUGE, is finally in place, like really in place! On May 21, 2019, it is confirmed that my birth name is Calissa. WOW!

It may not seem like much, but for me it was like a brick wall had finally fallen down and exposed sunlight and a cloudless sky. Someone actually knew some of the pieces floating around in my head! You have no idea, but this was a major breakthrough.

The weekend of my brother's birthday, which was Memorial Day weekend; his birthday is May 25 and we're the same age. I am older by a couple of months, but don't know exactly what that month is. And I'll explain how I got to that revelation. But I asked my brother; we were in the car together, and I'm taking him out for a night of birthday celebrations. "Who named you? Who named you and your little sister?"

And he was like, "our father named us."

And I said, "are you sure? Like your mom didn't have any say so, like nothing," and he was like, "No."

He was, "no, no, she didn't have no say so; my father, or our father, named us".

I said, "Okay."

So the fact my initials are CC, Calissa Cross, definitely raises an eyebrow that my father could have named me as well. He could have been at the hospital when I was born. I found it very interesting that there is still no birth certificate that has shown up yet for me with any version of my birth name.

One more reason for him to actually sit down and talk this out… so I can get answers I have been searching for decades… but that ship has sailed. I told him what I thought about him and he is now dead to me.

CHAPTER SEVENTEEN

....

My Mother's Side
of The Family

So after about a month and a half of connecting with my biological father's side of the family, and just being really devastated by the responses, I took a break. It is easy, once so much work has been done to move forward, to get really depressed when the response to it is negative. Irrespective, deep down, I realize I have to shake it off and I have to keep going toward my goal. But then, at the end of May, going into June, I reached out to Virginia, my search Angel, and was like okay, I'm ready to get back into it. So we started looking at my matches on 23andme, family heritage, and DNA ancestry, and I want to say it might have been 23andme that showed a second cousin who was a very, very, very close match. It clearly wasn't on my father's side because we were able to differentiate between the two and created the family tree.

So, Virginia and I ended up connecting those dots, reaching out to another family member who clearly wasn't on my father's side, (but wasn't for sure who they were, and what the relationship actually was). They immediately responded that would be Brian Thomas, my cousin. So, the search for my mom on the maternal side moved quite quickly.

On May 21, Brian reached out. "Great news. We were able to make contact with your Aunt Marilyn, and Joyce is your mother. Marilyn's phone number is xxx-xxxx and the best time to get her today is after 2pm".

He shared with me that Marilyn raised me for a while with her girls and, get this, she has another picture of me when I was younger, with her own daughters. This was at 9:40 on the day of May 21. As I was getting off the elevator heading into work, my knees collapsed and just gave out, and I just started crying. I was like, I finally found my mom! I'm getting off the elevator. I'm trying to walk into my office and I can barely stand up. I can barely walk and I'm just sobbing so hard. I walk into my office and I had to let the staff know we were going to have to reschedule the training; I ended up asking Brian to call me just to reassure me of everything so far. We talked for a few minutes since he was working and I was in awe and disbelief.

I went to a work appointment, despite being unable to fully concentrate. When I finished my appointment, I called Marilyn, my aunt, for the first time I was getting on the interstate; I was stuck in traffic. When I called her, my Aunt Marilyn answered the phone, and I was like, "Is this Marilyn?"... and she was like, "Calissa, we've been looking all over for you. Praise Jehovah! I'm so glad to be talking to you." And I just broke down crying again. I was crying so hard; I could barely see the traffic in front of me. I ended up having to pull over. No one has ever called me by my biological name. I never even knew my biological name. I just knew Calissa was the name I entered into state custody. And even though it was throughout my adoption file, it wasn't spelled correctly. It has been spelled all kinds of different ways. So, I wasn't sure if that was really my name, or if that was just the name someone gave me, or what, but to hear my aunt call me by my given name for the very first time was, oh my gosh, it was just a whole other feeling that I've never felt before.

And it might have been about three o'clock at that point. I think when I finished my appointment and pretty much from three o'clock that afternoon until probably after midnight, I was on the phone with her, her kids, uncles, other cousins, all on three-way conversations going back and forth. Everyone talking, everyone wanting to know where I was, what was going on with me, talking about my mom and all those things. I mean it was just the same way I'm exalting right now, is the exact same feeling I had back on that day, May 21. Being able to breathe, man. It's almost like I didn't even know I was suffocating. Or just maybe that I was even holding my breath this whole time. I mean it's a day I will never forget!

CHAPTER EIGHTEEN

....

Cautious Forward Movement

So, after connecting with my mom's side of the family, they were trying to protect me and they were cautious about things they told me upon my initial conversations with them and in future conversations I had with them too. They hadn't seen my mom in years. Wham! I don't know what I expected, but it was certainly a punch in the gut.

They expected she had passed away based on the word on the streets, but the actual truth was unknown. No one had a death certificate. No one knew where she was buried. No one knew what could have happened to her or anything. They just honestly believed she was deceased. And, of course, I was like, well, as I'm getting information from them, I knew I had her name, her date of birth. I'm kind of passing this information along to Virginia, my search Angel, and she's doing her due diligence with the search for my mom and any records of her, as well as searching for my birth certificate.

Now we know my name is Calissa Jones or Cross – after all these years I now know my real name! It was just an overload of information. Something that really, really, really stuck out was as they were talking, they were thinking that oh, we knew you were being raised by your father. That's what grandma used to tell us. You know, that's what your mom used to say, blah, blah, blah, blah. And I realized that wasn't true, but that's what they had been told. And that's what they had been believing all this time. So, I'm just kind of listening to them. And then when I finally got a moment to interject into the conversation, because I didn't want to interrupt them, I just wanted to hear all the info they had to share...

So, I ended up asking, "so, you guys knew my father and met him?" Now keep in mind, I already have had conversations with my father. I knew who he was. My brother had shared a lot of information. So my cousins were like, we might have met him, but we were so young. They couldn't really put a picture with a face or a face with a name. These two cousins who are sisters, they were going back and forth and I didn't even tell you this, but the big kicker was they were like where is Tashenia? And I was like, "who is that"? And they said, "that's your sister". This is just too much... really wild! And I didn't know I had a sister on my mom's side. Buckle in for another ride on the roller coaster!

And so now I am learning I have an older sister on my mom's side whom I am just now hearing about. But these cousins knew her and were raised with her for a period of time. The two cousins who are sisters, we're having a conversation while I'm on the phone with them, and they were talking about whose father was who. They're just kind of going back and forth and I'm just sitting back listening and not really giving any information because what I've learned in the past of putting too much information out there. I would just listen, you know, instead of giving any information until I felt like the time was right, so as the sisters are going back and forth, and it was like, your father's name is Clarence, and he drove for the Metro in New York. And if they hadn't hit the nail on the head, I'm just like, yeah, my father's name is Clarence. And yes, he did drive for the Metro and he retired from doing that. So everything they said was very accurate.

Why is my father claiming he never knew my mom or knew there was another child out there, but my mom's side of the family knew him? It brought up all kinds of other emotions for me, but I had to table that during this call. Then I shared with them how I grew up. In foster care, got adopted, then emancipated, and now, here I am.

It was their turn to break down, crying, not even knowing that I grew up in foster care. That was a shock for them. It was really, really interesting those conversations, those initial conversations of me connecting with my mom's side of the family, so I kind of savored those conversations and every day I talked to my mom's side of the family on top of talking to my brother on my dad's side of the family, because he is the closest one, the person that I was the closest to on my dad's side.

July was a very big month for me. I planned to go visit my mom's side of the family for the July 4th holiday; I took four days and went to Richmond, Virginia, which is where my Aunt Marilyn and my cousins lived, whom I had been interacting with daily. Since we connected back in May, I got to see them for the first time and spent the holidays with them. I met all of them, we talked and just caught up, and it was a really good feeling.

It was very hard to leave them. It was another emotional day for me when I left to get on my flight and I broke down because I was scared I wouldn't see my family anymore, and I had spent my whole entire life looking for family. And still knowing my mom could be somewhere out there because until we have documentation and proof, I was like, I'm still looking for this lady, you know. So that was the July 4th holiday and then gosh, I can't remember if they came down to visit me shortly after, or if I went to go see my father first. Anyway, this was all in July. Not only did I go meet my mom's side of the family, they all came down to Atlanta, my adopted brothers Michael and James, they came up from Tampa and my biological brother on my dad's side all came and we had a whole weekend of hanging out, getting to know one another. My family stayed with me. It was just a really good weekend.

Which was also the weekend I met my now husband. It must have been after that time I went to go see my dad which was also in July of that year.

CHAPTER NINETEEN

Taking It All In, My New Family

Moving forward from July 2019, I was just all over the place. I had new family members. I had two new sisters and a new brother on my biological father's side. I knew I had an older sister, and maybe a younger brother on my mom's side. That was a lot to digest. You know? I still hadn't found my mom. My mom's side of the family told me I had the siblings, and I knew I didn't have the energy to actively search for and engage with them.

My mom's side of the family had no additional information on my siblings. They just knew the names. Their first names, but didn't know the spelling, didn't know birth dates, or anything like that. So, I just knew I couldn't take that on right now. So I just put a pin in that. On my dad's side, I had two sisters, one older, who still lives in New York, and one who is younger; she is in the Navy. It was a lot of processing, all the emotions, all the feelings, you know, they were unaware of me. So this definitely caused a ripple in the family. However, this was proof that my biological father was cheating. The oldest sister had a different mom and the younger sister and the brother share the same mom who is still alive, and with whom my brother lives. And even though they have been divorced, and he has since remarried and then divorced again, even their mom had feelings about knowing her husband at the time had cheated on her.

And technically, my brother and I are the same age. We're really just maybe about a month and a half apart, if that. Still not sure when my actual birthday is, even to this date. The sisters weren't really welcoming or reaching out to me, so that was a very interesting thing. And so the rest of 2019 was, well, it was a little tough.

I'm learning about all kinds of new family members, cousins, aunts, uncles; learning things about my mom and who she was and things they had experienced with her. When I say they, it's really more on my mom's side because my dad is still standing behind the idea that he does not know my mom. And of course, none of my siblings on my dad's side knew of her or anything like that.

I'm going to say that in 2020, had to be towards the beginning of the year, maybe February of 2020, I think it was before the pandemic hit, I was hanging out with some cousins who were on my brother's mom's side because they wanted to meet me. I look exactly like my dad, of all his kids, I resemble him the most. But I had built relationships with some of the cousins even though they were kind of like ex cousins, I guess, because the wife had divorced the husband, my dad.

Relationships were built and one of the cousins, we're just kind of like hanging out having drinks and she tells me that my father had come into town and they had all caught COVID. My dad had COVID and she's telling me about the whole thing and I'm like, my dad was in town, and my brother and his mom live about 20 minutes at the most from me? 20 minutes?! Actually, the last time I spoke to him he said he was going to come to Atlanta and he never did, and since then we have not really spoken. As this cousin was telling me that my dad was in town and she didn't even know that I did not know? So, I'm just listening to her and processing it. We ended up wrapping up having drinks and went on about our way and as soon as I got home I spazzed out.

And when I say spazzed out; my emotions, the anger, I just was all over the place. It had hit the roof. I couldn't believe my dad was in town, I couldn't believe my brother hadn't told me. I couldn't believe no one had said anything. I could have gone over there and met him. So that threw me into a downward tailspin. I mean, I was angry. I wanted to hurt people. I didn't know why I was here anymore. I didn't know whether I wanted to be here anymore. I didn't want them here anymore. There was all kinds of emotions going on. It took me weeks to escape from those feeling, and I ended up having to find a therapist. And that's when I started my journey with my therapist. So, in 2020 I was just on this emotional roller coaster with family, like just trying to connect with siblings who wanted to connect you know, trying to feel them out, you know, fingers being pointed at me like I was the bad guy, and not really understanding what to do, then trying to get everyone to talk to my father, so that he would talk to me, and it was just a lot. It was a lot on top of Covid.

And 2021 was a busy year. A year of healing. Gosh, in 2021 I was still seeing my therapist virtually every single week. I was moving deeper into my family dynamics and learning more about them. And I started to dig deeper on trying to find my mom; I felt like I had unfinished business. I KNEW I had unfinished business. I found all these other family members and I was super excited about it, but my mom is still the big missing piece of the puzzle. And I need to find her. I said I wasn't worried about the other siblings on my mom's side because I knew I didn't have energy to do that. So my focus had turned to just finding my mom and figuring out my birth certificate.

In the summer of 2021, an uncle on my mom's side ended up passing away. And It's so crazy how I'm big on family even though I didn't really have that family bond and connection growing up. So, I went to events even during COVID in 2021. I went to family functions. I went to my brother's events on my dad's side. When the younger sister came into town, I just popped up over there at the house; I didn't wait for an invitation, and I didn't really even get an invitation, but I was able to meet her and other family members. I always made every effort to jump on a plane or drive to whatever the family had going on because I had missed out on so much.

I was there and I just wanted to be around my family after all these years, and I didn't want to lose them. So, knowing that my uncle had passed, who was one of my mom's oldest siblings, I was like, I gotta be there. So I ended up making some connections and finding his kids and connecting those dots. The funeral was planned. I was like, I'm going to New York. This would be my first time going to New York. I'm armed with all this information and all this research and all this content that I've received from family members. So, I started putting the pieces together, and I knew I wasn't gonna go to New York without looking for my mom. This was an opportunity for me to have boots on the ground. So, I have another uncle, Uncle Kenny, who lives in New York who was very close to the uncle who passed away; they were brothers, they were siblings.

Uncle Kenny put his ear to the ground and reached out to people in the Bronx neighborhood that he was looking for his sister. He ended up getting information back that his sister, my mom, might have gone underground using a different name. He eventually found out what that name was, so we started tracking that information. And I say we, meaning my search Angel and people from DNA detectives, and some of these other search groups who were very helpful. And so when I went to New York, I was prepared. I had my Google number written down, on maybe about 50 little sheets of paper to pass out. I had pictures of this alleged mom of mine that someone had given to my uncle, and I hit the ground running. I flew into New York before the rest of the family got in for my Uncle Ronald's memorial service. I walked the streets of the Bronx. When I tell you, I parked, and I just walked and I don't know what possessed me to do that. But I walked and walked, and I talked to people. I asked questions. I passed my number out. I'm looking for a woman in a wheelchair because they remembered my mom being in an accident and her not walking well.

And my Uncle Ronald, the one who passed away, used to push her in a wheelchair.

People were very helpful. They spoke to me; they gave me information. They guided me. I hadn't met my Uncle Kenny yet, but he was meeting me later that day when he had wrapped up some appointments. I had checked on my Uncle Ronald's funeral arrangements; I ended up parking right at the funeral home and that was a whole debacle. Just know that burying our Uncle Ronald was a very traumatic situation; the funeral home didn't do what they were supposed to do. And I think that was my biological mom's side of the family's first time seeing how I moved in action with handling business. Not only my Uncle Ronald's business, but my mom's business as well.

So I went to the hospitals and clinics all over the Bronx. All while trying to figure out if vital records will provide me with any information that would be helpful. I've walked for hours in the sun. This was August of 2021, so you know it was hot in those streets. And needless to say, it wasn't a successful trip. I wasn't able to find my mom, and it was very traumatic. The woman I was searching for was not my mom. It turns out that I had information that was given to me by family members that was inaccurate. But the researcher in me, I'm gonna exhaust all spectrums of everything. And that's what I did. I was beyond exhausted; physically, mentally, emotionally; I overdid it.

I did find this lady who was in a wheelchair who was supposed to be whatever her name was; this alias they thought was my mom, but it was really another woman. And on the day we connected with her, was the day we were burying my uncle, and the whole family came with me to meet her. The family went to meet her first because they would be the ones who would be able to identify her, because I've never seen my mom since I was an infant. So, they went and some family members thought it was her, but the majority of the other family members thought she was not my mom.

By the end of it all, turns out she wasn't my mom. A very shady character, to be sure, but the family had identified her as not being related to us. We left her feeling defeated; I was empty. I could barely walk or think any more. I went straight to the airport and went home completely beaten down.

CHAPTER TWENTY

The End... For Now

That trip to New York in August 2021, was extremely traumatic for me. I learned a lot from that trip even though I didn't find my mom. I was a walking zombie after that trip and could not even explain to my then boyfriend, Steven, now my husband, what all I went through. I could write a book just on that trip alone. So there were many, many details I left out and probably for the better.

I didn't realize when I was leaving New York I had spent my whole entire life searching for my parents, like forget siblings and other family members, but I had been searching for my parents and to get so freakin close... And to be dealing with this stuff like I just couldn't process what my purpose was anymore. I didn't know why I was supposed to be here. I didn't know what I was supposed to do next.

And this makes me very emotional right now, because I didn't want to live anymore. I just wanted to crawl up in a corner and disconnect from all this new family, disconnect from everything going on. It was just hard. I was tired of pushing and I was tired of being the bigger person. I was tired of doing all this stuff to find my family and then to be treated a certain way, and then to find out certain information wasn't even valid. Like it almost took me OUT! But my God is an on-time God! A week after the New York trip, Steven and I had a vacation booked. And that just so happens to have been the vacation that he proposed to me, so yeah, timing. It was exactly what I needed because I didn't know what to do next.

It was almost like God saying, 'I've allowed you to go on this journey for all these years. I've given you room. I've given you time. I've given you the space to find your family. Now it's time for you to move on to this next chapter'. And it was also a moment of me realizing that whatever happened, God knew what He was doing with me from initially being born, from the time I was an infant, and being given away or given up or stolen, or whatever the fuck happened, like God knew what He was doing then, but he still allowed me to go on this journey. And then God saying like, 'I'm picking you up, and it's time for you to move on to this chapter, to become a wife and create your OWN family'.

And so now, I have a family, stuff I never thought I could have, because I felt like I was so broken that I didn't belong anywhere, because I didn't fit in anywhere… God put this man in my life who pretty much told me he loved me, no matter what, and I finally felt like I had found unconditional love. I was like wow, this guy does really love me, it's not the love that I have previously experienced all these years, or the lack thereof.

So, at that point from being engaged and planning a wedding, I think we got married eight months later. And it felt so good to have such much of my family at my wedding. I did noy have any of my biological dad's side because I really had to put some boundaries in place to deal with my biological dad's side. My brother hurt me, while not intentionally, but it was because he didn't know what to do. You know the sisters; they just were mean and disconnected from me. The dad that I still have not met, there was just so much hurt there that I was like I couldn't allow that into this next chapter of my life. So they weren't at my wedding, but my mom's side was, my adoptive family was, my friends, and it was beautiful. I still have a desire to search for my mom and to search for my sibling(s) that are still missing. But, at that time, I was like, let me just embrace being married and start creating the life that I've always wanted (thanks Alisha), even though I felt like I didn't deserve, or I hadn't earned it or that it wasn't for me, you know?

Life never stops, that is for sure. In February of 2023, I connected with my biological big sister on my mom's side, and I learned a whole lot more about my mom. This big sister was there when I was born. She knew me and she remembers when I disappeared. We have a beautiful relationship now and have seen each other several times this year already. Because she was older she remembers a lot more. And she has great memories about our mom, and then there's some not so good memories. So we've been able to connect on that level and we did work a little bit on my mom. And it's believed that our mom is potentially deceased, and maybe listed as a 'Jane Doe'.

We have met with the chief medical examiner for New York; they have collected our DNA and we are waiting on results to come back to compare nationally to any Jane Doe in the country.

After meeting my sister in February, my husband and I celebrated our one-year anniversary with the news of a baby on board! For us, 2023 has been quite a year! Every year has been a revelation, some years more than we could handle, other years not as difficult, but here we are and still in one piece!

We have had many monumental losses with family and loved ones. But I am still pressing forward. It hurts that the only 'dad' I knew is now gone. My husband's parents are gone. My biological mom is unaccounted for and my biological dad has yet to connect back with me.

It still hurts as I've had to heal from the trauma of being rejected. Not being accepted, feeling like it's my fault and just all kinds of stuff with my biological dad. It still hurts that he doesn't want to have a relationship with me and I have had to learn that it's not me, it's him, and these are his own demons he is fighting and struggling with. And whether he wants to face it or not, I am his child. And then knowing my mom is not present. Yet, my heart is full.

We do have a lot of family and friends' support from our tribe.

You know, baby Bailey is baking in this oven and will be here soon. And yeah, I'm looking forward to this book and what it's gonna be, and I mean I've experienced so many emotions as I've been writing it.

So, with that being said, I know I still have work to do. Thank you for reading my journey. Thank you for allowing me to share what's Beneath This Smile, and being incredibly vulnerable with the pieces of my life, some of which are not so glamorous. Thank you, Universe, for letting me find peace, at least for this moment in time.

ACKNOWLEDGEMENTS

To my husband, Steven... THANK you for allowing me to be ME and for loving me just as I am. You opened so many doors inside of me and filled them with LOVE. Thank you for our beautiful family and for never wavering.

My brothers, Michael & James... Thank you for choosing me to be your sister and never giving up on me.

Dorothy and the late Michael Branham, Sr... Thank you for allowing me to be a part of your family and raising me the only way you knew how.

KP... from the countless calls pushing each other to stay focused, bounce ideas off, and pushing each other to new heights, Thank YOU.

To my search angel, Virginia... you mean so much to me. You gave me HOPE and never gave up. Thank you for all that YOU are to me and sooooo many others.

Alisha Walker... our paths crossed right on time and for that I am grateful.

To my biological family... I am grateful to have found each and every one of you. We won't worry about the past, but my smile is ever so big knowing that I have you all in my life.

I can't thank everyone individually, but to my TRIBE who has supported me along this journey, THANK YOU. I know I would not have come this far without the universe doing what it does. I truly feel honored and blessed to have come this far.

Simone Bailey

www.ingramcontent.com/pod-product-compliance
Lightning Source LLC
Chambersburg PA
CBHW021121130626
46554CB00002B/801